Charles M. Natoli

Nietzsche and Pascal on Christianity

PETER LANG

New York · Berne · Frankfurt am Main

Library of Congress Cataloging in Publication Data

Natoli, Charles M., 1949–
  Nietzsche and Pascal on Christianity.

  (American University Studies.   Series V, Philosophy;
v. 3)
  Bibliography: p.
  1. Nietzsche, Friedrich Wilhelm, 1844–1900 – Theology.
2. Pascal, Blaise, 1623–1662 – Theology.   3. Christianity
– 19th Century.   4. Christianity – 17th Century.
I. Title.   II. Series.
B3318.C35N37 1985   230   83-49020
ISBN 0-8204-0071-8
ISSN 0739-6392

CIP-Kurztitelaufnahme der Deutschen Bibliothek

Natoli, Charles M.:
Nietzsche and Pascal on Christianity / Charles M.
Natoli. – New York; Berne; Frankfurt am Main: Lang, 1985.
  (American University Studies: Ser. 5, Philosophy;
  Vol. 3)
  ISBN 0-8204-0071-8

NE: American University Studies / 05

B
3318
. C35
N37
1985

© Peter Lang Publishing, Inc., New York 1985

Printed by Lang Druck, Inc., Liebefeld/Berne (Switzerland)

Certo a colui che meco s'assottiglia,
se la Scrittura sovra voi non fosse,
da dubitar sarebbe a maraviglia.

Dante, *Paradiso*, XIX

Table of Contents

ACKNOWLEDGMENTS

I have incurred many debts in the writing of this book and I should like to express my thanks to all who have helped me. Ralph McInerny directed an earlier, substantially different version that served as my doctoral thesis at the University of Notre Dame. Alasdair MacIntyre read a substantial part of the present manuscript while I attended the NEH Summer Seminar he headed at Wellesley College. Both were more than helpful. However, special thanks are due to Kurt and Florence Weinberg, each of whom offered detailed and searching comments on a goodly portion of the manuscript. I made free use of their suggestions in the final draft and even slavishly copied a few turns of phrase it would have been folly to tamper with.

It need hardly be added that I am wholly responsible for any errors in the final product, and that those who have helped me cannot be taken to agree with all that it contains. Far from it!

Pascal scholarship, especially that concerned with the *Pensées*, is almost a field study in its own right. My own acquaintance with it owes much to the works of Patricia Topliss and even more to those of Louis Lafuma and Jean Mesnard. I have made liberal use of the works of all three.

I would like to thank the following publishers for permission to quote from their translations: Cambridge University Press for Nietzsche's *Daybreak*, tr. by R.J. Hollingdale (1982); Random House for Nietzsche's *The Birth of Tragedy and The Case of Wagner*, tr. by Walter Kaufmann (1966); Nietzsche's *Beyond Good and Evil*, tr. by Walter Kaufmann (1966); Nietzsche's *The Will to Power*, ed. by Walter Kaufmann and tr. by Walter Kaufmann and

R.J. Hollingdale (1967); Nietzsche's *On The Genealogy of Morals*, translated by Walter Kaufmann and R.J. Hollingdale, and *Ecce Homo*, tr. by Walter Kaufmann (1968); and Penguin Books, Ltd., for Pascal's *Pensées*, tr. by A.J. Krailsheimer, © A.J. Krailsheimer, 1966; Nietzsche's *The Twilight of the Idols and The Anti-Christ*, tr. by R.J. Hollingdale, © R.J. Hollingdale 1968; and Nietzsche's *Thus Spoke Zarathustra*, tr. by R.J. Hollingdale, © R.J. Hollingdale 1961, 1969. The last four titles appeared at Harmondsworth, Middlesex in the Penguin Classics series; excerpts therefrom are reprinted by permission of Penguin Books, Ltd.

Several friends, and in particular my wife, Joanna, graciously helped with the proofs.

Finally, I would like to express my gratitude to the National Endowment for the Humanities and to my own institution, St. John Fisher College, for grants that made the completion of this study possible.

A Note on Citations

Following Walter Kaufmann, I have used the following abbreviations for works of Nietzsche:

Die Geburt der Tragödie (The Birth of Tragedy)	1872	GT

Unzeitgemässe Betrachtungen (Untimely Meditations)   U

   I *David Strauss, der Bekenner und Schriftsteller*   1873
(David Strauss, the Confessor and Writer)

  II *Vom Nutzen und Nachteil der Historie für das*   1874
Leben (Of the Use and Disadvantage of History for Life)

 III *Schopenhauer als Erzieher* (Schopenhauer as   1874
Educator)

 IV *Richard Wagner in Bayreuth*   1876

Menschliches, Allzumenschliches (Human, All-Too   MA
Human)

  I   1878

  II *Vermischte Meinungen und Sprüche* (Mixed 1879
Opinions and Maxims)

Der Wanderer und sein Schatten (The Wanderer 1880 S
and His Shadow)

Die Morgenröte (The Dawn)   1881 M

Die Fröhliche Wissenschaft (The Gay Science) 1882 FW
Book V (s. 343–383) added in 1887.

Also Sprach Zarathustra (Thus Spoke Zarathustra) 1883–5 Z

Jenseits von Gut und Böse (Beyond Good and Evil) 1886 J

Zur Genealogie der Moral (On the Genealogy of 1887 GM
Morals)

Der Fall Wagner (The Case of Wagner) 1888 W

Die Götzen-Dämmerung (The Twilight of the 1889 G
Idols)

Der Antichrist (The Antichrist) 1895* A

Ecce Homo Contains four chapters plus ten sec- 1908* EH
tions on works above, e.g., EH-Z.

Nietzsche Contra Wagner Ten chapters. 1895* NCW

Der Wille zur Macht (The Will to Power) Not a 1901* WM
book of N's but a selection of material from his
notebooks published after his death.

Vorreden (Prefaces) are abbreviated "V", e.g., J-V.
Epilog is abbreviated "Ep"; e.g., W-Ep.

Works whose date is marked with an asterisk appeared posthumously. Volume and page references not preceded by a letter

abbreviation are to the *Gesammelte Werke, Musarionausgabe* (23 vols., Munich, 1920—29). Unless otherwise indicated, all other references to his works are by section number; these are the same in all editions. With few exceptions, works prior to M are quoted in the translation of the Oscar Levy edition, *The Complete Works of Friedrich Nietzsche* (New York: 1909—1911). Works after and including M are quoted in the translations of Walter Kaufmann and/or R.J. Hollingdale.

I have used the following abbreviations for Pascal:

Oeuvres Complètes (Paris: Éditions du Seuil, 1963),   OC
ed. Louis Lafuma.

Pensées (The edition used throughout is that of Lafuma
in OC.)   P

References to the *Pensées* are to the number assigned to the individual fragment (*pensée*). The numeration of the fragments varies greatly from edition to edition. Lafuma's numeration in OC is now the standard one although Brunschvicg's edition with its different numeration still has many adherents. A concordance between the Lafuma and Brunschvicg editions is found in OC. The problems involved in presenting the *Pensées* and the principles underlying a number of editions are discussed in chapter one.

Quotations from the *Pensées* are given in the Penguin Classics translation of A.J. Krailsheimer (1967). His numeration is that of OC.

I have thought fit to make a few small modifications in some of the translations cited. Unattributed translations are my own.

In the footnotes, works are cited in full on their first appearance only; afterwards they are designated by author only or by abbreviated title. There is a Select Bibliography at the end of the volume which contains all works cited on Nietzsche and/or Pascal.

PREFACE

This book springs from and reflects a variety of convictions. The chief among them are that adult religious belief demands rational scrutiny; that a "heaving bosom" is no reason for anyone not resigned to perpetual intellectual minority; that the standard of rationality used to measure religious faith is itself far from given, fixed and unproblematic; that Nietzsche and Pascal represent, not incidentally opposed though historically related positions on Christianity, but fundamentally and instructively contrasting approaches to the problems it poses; that Nietzsche's anti-Christian polemics, the most vitriolic and shrill of recent times, are far from mere bluster and deserve to be considered carefully; and that, contrary to the milennia-old "party line," the compatibility of reason with the "Mysteries" of traditional Christian belief is not apparent — quite the reverse — and that this, together with the consequent options for the orthodox believer, should be squarely confronted and deliberately considered.

Three other points by way of preamble would be useful to the reader.

First, I discuss "Christianity" as something of an abstraction, a set of propositions culled from the Scriptures and creeds and from orthodox theology and its handmaid, and not, as some might, as a *practice* playing diverse roles in the life of believers, or again as an institution. What is believed is propositions, not practices or institutions, and the foundations of these latter are rooted in a set of beliefs. Furthermore, I have tried not to represent orthodox Christian belief in terms peculiar to any particular sect, but even with some controversial doctrines omitted, it

15

goes without saying that not all who call themselves Christians would subscribe to "orthodoxy" as I define it. I have nonetheless tried to represent what I take the common belief-heritage of Christians to be.

Secondly, owing to the wide interest in the issues under discussion, I have sought to make this book intelligible not only to professional philosophers but also to the philosophically apt. Inevitably, this has resulted in occasional notes or explanations which are redundant for the professional. I think nevertheless that neither audience will find it profitless, though the latter may find the going tough in a few places.

Finally, I should advise both sets of readers that this book is less an attempt to break new ground than an endeavor to show that, despite current enthusiasm for some of the new digs, many of the old ones have been abandoned far too soon. (Given the rocklike consistency of the ground, this is not wholly surprising.) The fact is, I think, that many of the old problems with Christian belief either await definitive resolution — and maybe nothing short of the lightnings of the Last Day could bring this — or else are resolved or resolvable at a price not fully realized.

INTRODUCTION

Shortly after I had formulated my intention of writing a book on Nietzsche and Pascal, an eminent academician of my acquaintance (who shall remain nameless) asked me why I had chosen to treat *them* together. "Why not write on Thales and Kant?" he jested. I cannot answer for the reasonableness of that project, but there is much to be said for treating Nietzsche and Pascal in tandem.

First of all, there are sound historical reasons for doing so. Nietzsche was a great reader of Pascal throughout his adult life. References to him abound in his works, almost all of them favorable — a fact at first glance surprising given the radical disparity between their views. Pascal is an ascetic; Nietzsche sees in asceticism a crime against life, a No! to it. Pascal is a devout Christian; he is thus a member of a creed Nietzsche holds in unparalleled disdain, loosing against it searing anathemas. And yet, as we shall see, in a curious way they were (to borrow a term from Trinitarian theology) *homoousios*, of the same substance, a fact Nietzsche recognized when he said that Pascal's blood ran in his veins (XXI, 98). Thus, their relationship is a fair field for the historian of ideas intent on studying the information of this common substance by Nietzschean accidents — a phenomenon which produced the most intriguing results — and intent on gauging Nietzsche's debts to Pascal.

In addition, there are quasi-aesthetic reasons for treating them together. A study of the contrasts and affinities between two such richly exotic specimens of human fauna will interest the philosopher in the large sense, the connoisseur of what is best and most remarkable in the type man. Or, in other words, such a study will

17

interest anyone who is at all like Nietzsche. And of course Pascal and Nietzsche are of interest to connoisseurs of the human spirit for their penetrating analyses of its fortes and foibles as well as on their own account.

Both saw man uncommonly — and uncomfortably — clearly, and both are such strange, inexhaustible geniuses that to see them clearly is neither so common nor so comfortable. Their depths are not discernible at a glance, and their uncompromising intensity discomfits. We are, most of us, too tolerant, too latitudinarian to be at ease in the presence of men who insist that they have penetrated to the truth of things. And we are even less at ease when, as both aver, the truth is that man as he is is sadly deficient and not easily bettered.

But what is most important in the study of these two is that the tensions between and in their philosophies present us with problems of an interest all their own, questions as fundamental as they are elusive of exact resolution. Is man a thing of great or little worth? Are one's vital instincts something to exult in or to overcome? Is Christianity a way to salvation or what we need salvation from? And is the *value* of a conception of more importance than its *truth*? This last question is a remarkable one in its own right and a crucial one for understanding the Nietzsche/Pascal relationship. Both were preoccupied with Christianity, but their approaches to it differ no less than their eventual conclusions. Pascal agonizes over its truth. If he can, he will prove it to the *libertin*, the *honnête homme*, the urbane, educated, worldly skeptic. And, I think, to himself. Nietzsche, on the other hand, focuses on the value of Christianity's effects on the type man. This is in keeping with his startling view, set forth and discussed in chapters three and four, that a conception's value is more important than its truth.

18

Historically-minded criticism of ideas too often degenerates into after the fact biographical explanations of the ideas' supposed genesis. This, in addition to trivializing the ideas, ignores the truth set forth by Proust in *Contre Sainte-Beuve* that a great work is the product of "*un autre moi*" than the fellow accessible to friends and biographers. Yet failure to appreciate the historical context of arguments often reduces them to "straw men." Every age has assumptions peculiar to it which are almost universally affirmed and hence seldom made explicit. Thus even the most ahistorically-minded analytic philosopher must look to the man and his time occasionally to give his author's arguments a fair hearing; no argument is without a context. I have tried to avoid the twin shoals of considering arguments as though they were authorless and of doing what Jaspers did in a fine book of its type on Nietzsche — giving pride of place to the man and his philosophizing rather than to his philosophy. Above all, I have tried to set forth and assess Nietzsche's and Pascal's ideas on Christianity.

Three things should be said at this point regarding the course I have chosen.

First of all, anyone who attempts a close analysis of Nietzsche's arguments may seem liable to a charge of Philistinism. On a certain view, Nietzsche was a poet in prose, a spectacular artist, fecund in intoxicating ideas which, owing to his sovereign contempt for systems, he did not fully develop and which therefore naturally exhibit some tensions ("contradictions" to less receptive readers). To scrutinize the epistemology of such an eccentric genius (as I have done) is the part of a churl abhorred of the Muses. To use Baudelaire's famous figure, the graceful, free-flying albatross is dragged down to earth where the great wings which enabled him to soar so well now make walking difficult and earn him the jeers of the earthbound.

Such a "defense" of Nietzsche has no merit. It disregards the plain fact that he thought he was absolutely right in what he said. Indeed, he accompanies the exposition of his doctrines with hymns of praise for their acuity and of thanksgiving for the havoc they wreak on error; it is a continual *Te Deum* which verges on *taedium*. But, more importantly, it is a flat-out insult to Nietzsche to suggest that his ideas are not worth taking seriously, that *of course* they will not withstand sustained analysis, that they are of interest primarily for their shock value, exoticism or illustration of his proto-modernity. I am no more unmusical (in the strict sense) than the next man, but I utterly reject this approach; its condescension and impertinence to a man of Nietzsche's stature are insufferable.

Secondly, the reader will note that I deal with Nietzsche at greater length than Pascal and criticize him at much greater length. Both effects have the same cause: I am in fundamental agreement with Pascal on many more issues. Hence, I have thought it proper not to try the reader's patience by continually recording my assent but rather to focus on what I thought was problematic.

This does not mean that I am insensitive to the many problems with Pascal's apologetics. Nor would I engage the reader *en abyme* with an Apology for his Apology. We differ on many points, and I do not find in him an answer to many of the problems with Christian belief raised in the Appendix. Yet I am profoundly impressed with the verisimilitude of his case for Christian theism. And like him, I am impressed by the case for skepticism because, like Kant and others, I am troubled by the confrontation of reason with antinomies. Like Bayle and Unamuno, I am of the minority that sees the essential doctrines of the Christian faith as essentially contra-rational, not merely supra-rational. But, perhaps like a fool, I do not find this to be *necessarily* a decisive objection to them.

20

Finally, it has seemed to me that a detailed exposition of Pascal's and Nietzsche's views on Christianity was called for if they were to be properly appreciated. The main lines of their positions are well known, but their arrangement and emphases are another matter.

Nietzsche's style is often aphoristic, especially in the earlier works, and sometimes oracular, as in *Thus Spoke Zarathustra*. Moreover, his complete position on Christianity is not to be found in any one work but must be pieced together from a number of them. Thus, the expositor's task is far from mechanical. One must try to connect loose ends in some contexts and unravel Gordian knots in others, to explain suggestive but Sibylline aphorisms and *obiter dicta* in the light of fuller passages and to condense fulsome tirades – all the while remaining faithful to the texts and the spirit of the man.

Pascal's position is even more difficult to arrive at – much more so, unfortunately. His *chef d'oeuvre* on behalf of Christianity, intended as an Apology but presented by editors simply as the *Pensées*, is fragmentary and unfinished. Not surprisingly, it is beset with a number of very knotty editorial and exegetical problems. And I might add that not all of the many distortions of Pascal's thought by his editors have been unwitting. These considerations have necessitated the inclusion of some prologomena to the study of the *Pensées* which I hope the reader will find valuable. They contain an editorial history and a review of the available evidence regarding the plan of Pascal's apologetic argument.

In the first chapter I have tried, not only to present Pascal's thought on Christianity to those unfamiliar with it, but to correct what are *pseudodoxia epidemica* even in the scholarly literature. The most notable are that the "wager" is meant to conclude in belief in the *Christian* God and that it is a "doomsday" argument

21

based on threats and menaces. The same is true to a lesser extent in the chapters on Nietzsche. There I argue against the views of some prominent commentators who hold that atheism is a conclusion, not an axiom, in Nietzsche's philosophy; that his critique of Christianity can be dismissed as a crass example of the genetic fallacy; and that, at bottom, his anti-Christian polemics sprung from motives that were basically Christian — that his, as some say of Plato's, was an *anima naturaliter Christiana*.

CHAPTER ONE

PASCAL'S APOLOGY FOR CHRISTIANITY

Pascal spent much of his short life meditating (some would say brooding) on Christian doctrine. He concluded that Christianity is true with regard to its metaphysical, historical and moral claims, and that it is of the utmost importance to assent to these truths and live by them. He spoke of two classes of men who have not discovered this. The first is composed of those who "seek with groans," who earnestly and diligently seek the truth and lament that they have not found it. They are deserving of our pity. Not so those who, either from sloth or indifference, make no effort to determine whether or not Christianity rests on solid foundations. One need not be pious to feel that they are well-nigh monstrous in their indifference to matters on which so much may hinge.

It is not over-bold to say that the adult Nietzsche belonged to the second class of unbeliever despite the length and virulence of his anti-Christian polemics. That Christianity might after all be true was a thought which seems to have intruded on his speculations but rarely if ever. This would hardly be surprising if he had spent most of his time pondering the metaphysical foundations of physical science or recent advances in mathematical logic. But it is odd given that Nietzsche was primarily a *moraliste* in the grand tradition of Montaigne, Pascal, La Rochefoucauld and Rousseau, and that Christianity, his *bête noire*, loomed large in his latest and best works. And yet, Nietzsche was a loving, long-time reader of Pascal. Why was he so insensitive to what was central for Pascal, the question of Christianity's truth?

In order to appreciate Nietzsche's reasons for parting company with him we need to know just what is to be found in Pascal. Why did he think that Christianity was true, and why did he think that it was absolutely essential to make the question of its truth *the* question, the one which at all costs must be met head-on? Pascal's answers to these queries are to be found in the *Pensées*, the chief locus of his apologetics and indeed of his religious thought as a whole. In this chapter I shall give an account of his case for Christianity as it survives in a more or less provisional form in that unfinished and fragmentary work.

Now one might ask, "Why is a new account of Pascal's apologetics necessary? Surely the Pascalian landscape has been so much surveyed and studied that even on the borders of the charts scarcely any *terra incognita* remains." In point of fact, however, most of the chartmakers have taken their bearings from the wrong stars. It is only in this century that, thanks largely to the researches of Tourneur and Lafuma, we possess a text in which it is possible to discern directly the movements of Pascal's mind and in which we are spared the obtrusiveness of the editor as much as is possible. And even when the editorial problems surrounding the *Pensées* are discounted, exegetical difficulties of a very knotty sort remain. After all, in any editorial arrangement Pascal's fragments are still fragments. Some work is required to discover their most likely inter-connections and to flesh out the more elliptical ones. Considering, then, the difficulties which abound in the reading of Pascal, it is necessary to bring the resources of modern scholarship to bear on our reading of him. Thus, we shall begin with a short editorial history of the *Pensées* and then consider such evidence as survives of Pascal's apologetic plans before giving

24

an account of his apologetics proper. Without such background information, the reader can have no idea why one account of Pascal's thought might be more faithful to his intentions than another. It is unfortunate but true that there is no short cut or "royal road" to the discovery of Pascal's apologetic plans. But it is both fortunate and true that the story of the *Pensées* is of interest in its own right. It might be thought of as a kind of picaresque novel in which an ill-starred orphan (the text) meets with manifold rogueries and misfortunes in a long string of episodic encounters.

A final word: I am of course fully aware that Nietzsche could not have read Pascal as we are about to read him here, that is, through the lens of contemporary scholarship. In this chapter, however, I am primarily concerned to elucidate what Pascal was really up to in his apologetics rather than merely what Nietzsche thought he was up to. After all, perhaps we, like Nietzsche, would do well to come to grips with Pascal, and there is no reason why we ought to see him exclusively through Nietzschean spectacles. What Nietzsche saw in Pascal and how he reacted to it is the subject of chapter three.

A Short History of the Pensées: An Iliad of Editorials Ills

Pascal once said that if Cleopatra's nose had been formed differently, the course of subsequent history might have been very different.[1] One could also illustrate the force of happenstance in events by observing that if Pascal's father had not fallen and broken his leg, the history of French literature, philosophy and theological controversy might have been other (and less) than it has proved to be. The reason is simply that but for Étienne Pascal's fall, Blaise Pascal might have been other than he was.

The Pascals – Étienne, the precocious Blaise and his sisters Gilberte and Jaqueline – had always been a fairly pious family of conventional Catholics. But in 1646, after Étienne's fall, they made the acquaintance of two pious bonesetters who introduced them to a certain M. Guillebert, the vicar of a local church and a disciple of St. Cyran.[2] The family soon came under the influence of this Jansenist[3] cleric, and under his guidance their piety became much more intense than before. Of all the family Blaise, already internationally known for his scientific and mathematical work,[4] seems to have been the most deeply affected.

And yet he was not touched so deeply as he was to be between ten-thirty and twelve-thirty on the night of November 23, 1654. On that *"nuit de feu"* the thirty-one year old Pascal underwent a kind of second conversion when it seemed that the "Hidden God" of Christianity revealed himself to him. Pascal recorded the experience on a piece of paper which is now called the "Memorial." He had a parchment copy sewn into the lining of one of his garments so that he could keep it about him at all times. "Fire," he wrote in large letters in the center of the page, "God of Abraham, God of Isaac, God of Jacob, not of philosophers and scholars."[5] This was the God Pascal fervently worshipped ever after. And needless to say it was this God, not the *quid nomenis* of some Scholastic argument, of whom he wrote in his unfinished Apology for the Christian religion. The bulk of the fragmentary *Pensées* forms a sort of provisional draft of this work.

In her *Vie de M. Pascal*, Gilberte Périer (her married name) relates that a miracle occurred among the Jansenist community in March, 1656.[6] Her daughter was suddenly cured of a lachrymal fistula after the application by touch of what was reputed to be one of the Holy Thorns. From that time on, she continues, her brother Blaise meditated much on miracles and soon began to collect materials for a reasoned defence of Christianity which would be based on them. By 1658, however, he had modified the plan of his Apology to include many things besides miracles. Unfortunately Pascal's health, always delicate, had so deteriorated by 1659 that he was forced to suspend work on the project for over a year. Even so, he managed to compose about one fourth of the jottings which make up the *Pensées* in the time between his resumed activity and his death in 1662.

When an idea came to Pascal he would jot it down on a large piece of paper marked with a cross at the top, writing sometimes along the length of the paper, sometimes along the width. He separated his jottings with horizontal lines drawn accross the page.

In 1658 he completed a preliminary classification of his material. He cut the papers along the horizontal lines and grouped the fragments, each containing a *pensée*, into *liasses* (bundles) which were held together by a string put through a hole in the fragments.

On examining Pascal's papers after his death, the Périer family found that 382 fragments had been sorted into twenty-seven *liasses*, each of which had been given a title or heading. These titles also appeared in a Table of Contents the autograph of which has been lost. The rest of the material was grouped in *liasses* which were without titles (save for one entitled "Miscellanea").[7] This material contains approximately six hundred fragments, some of which are drafts for the *Provincial Letters* and for a separate work

27

on miracles. A few *pensées* from other sources have come to light since the seventeenth century.[8]

Étienne Périer, Pascal's nephew, tells us that the family's first action was to have the fragments copied in the precise order in which they were found.[9] As a matter of fact, we have two copies of the *pensées* which the Périer family had made. Their orderings are not identical, and we have no *conclusive* way of showing which one represents the order of Pascal's papers exactly as they were found after his death. Fortunately, the similarities between the First and Second Copies are more important than their divergences.

The material found in the *liasses à titres* is grouped in exactly the same way in both Copies, that is, according to the Table of Contents which is found in both Copies. It is only the order of appearance of the *liasses sans titres* which differs, apart from the fact that the Second Copy contains one *liasse* (dealing with the fable of Esdras) not found in the First Copy.

It is customary to assign the *liasses à titres* Arabic numerals from 1 to 27 and to number the *liasses sans titres* XXVIII to XXXIV based on the order in which they appear in the First Copy. The *liasse* containing the fable of Esdras is assigned **XXXV**. Consequently, the composition of the First Copy (now ms. 9203 in the *fonds français* of the Bibliothèque Nationale) is of course 1 to 27, XXVIII to XXXIV. The Second Copy is constituted as follows:

$$
\begin{array}{ccc}
& \text{I} & \\
1 & \text{to} & 27 \\
& \text{XXXV} & \\
\text{XXXII} & \text{to} & \text{XXXIV} \\
\text{XXIII} & \text{to} & \text{XXXI} \\
\text{XXI} & \text{and} & \text{XXII} \\
& \text{XX} & \\
\text{II} & \text{to} & \text{XIX}
\end{array}
$$

28

XXXII to XXXIV deal with miracles while XXI and XXII concern *l'esprit*, particularly *l'esprit de finesse* and *l'esprit géométrique*. XX treats the problem of belief while XXXV, as was noted above, contains the Fable of Esdras. Presumably there are organizing principles underlying the other groupings, but they are not easy to ascertain.

For a time the Périer family debated whether or not to publish Pascal's papers at all, so little order and interconnection did they seem to contain. But at length, bowing to the wishes of Pascal's friends and admirers, it appointed a committee headed by the Duc de Roannez to see to their publication.[10]

In his *Préface* to the first edition of the *Pensées*, the Port-Royal edition of 1670, Étienne Périer, one of the committee members, tells us that three options were considered. The first was to print the papers in exactly the same order that Pascal had left them. This was not done on account of what seemed to the editors the extreme disorder of this arrangement. The second was to finish Pascal's Apology for him by completing obviously unfinished fragments and by ordering the ensemble according to what they knew of Pascal's designs. This project was long considered and even begun, but eventually it was abandoned as being too difficult. The third option consisted in making a selection from among what were considered to be the more finished fragments and arranging them for the reader. This the committee did.

One would naturally assume, as almost all editors of the *Pensées* until the mid nineteenth century did, that Pascal's family and the committee it appointed would be the best guides to his intentions and the most faithful expositors of his ideas. After all, they knew and loved Pascal and doubtless he had often discussed his plans for the Apology with them. Unfortunately, the committee fashioned a work which was very much its own, one in which care was taken to efface any sign of seeming heterodoxy. For this we have the word of one of its own members, Antoine Arnauld, in a letter to Florin Périer (Gilberte's husband):

> Allow me to say that one must not be so difficult nor so scrupulous (*religieux*) about leaving a work as it left the hands of the author when there are those who wish to expose it to public censure. One must not be too exact when one has to deal with enemies as nasty as ours. It is much better to prevent chicaneries by some little changes which only soften an expression than to reduce onself to the necessity of justifying things [later].[11]

It can hardly be said that "softening an expression" could be faithful to the intentions of the man who, as the author of the *Provincial Letters*, showed himself to be one of the greatest polemicists of his century. Also, even though the Port-Royal editors knew that Pascal was preparing an Apology, they left this word out of the title; they produced a work called *Pensées de M. Pascal sur la religion et sur quelques autres sujets, qui ont été trouvées après sa mort parmi ses papiers.* Furthermore, they printed a selection of fragments drawn largely from the *liasses sans titres* under thirty-two headings which, for the most part, were of their own invention.

This edition saw numerous reprintings. No new edition appeared until 1776 when Condorcet brought one out. In this strange compilation the *pensées* were selected and arranged so as to make Pascal, a very devout man indeed, appear to be an atheist and much more of a skeptic than ever he was. For instance, Article Three is entitled "That it would be necessary to believe in and practice the Christian religion, even when one cannot prove it" even though Pascal held that religion did have "proofs," albeit not demonstrative ones. And in the margin of fragment XXI of Article Two, one reads:

> People will not fail to accuse the editor, who has assembled these scattered *pensées*, of being an atheist, an enemy of all morality. But I beg the authors of this objection to consider that the *pensées* are Pascal's and not mine. If they are an atheist's, it is Pascal who was an atheist, and not I . . . .[12]

Although this edition set a mark for editorial distortion of the *Pensées* not reached before or since — Voltaire, in letters to d'Alembert and de Vaines, commended it as *"l'anti-Pascal"* — it seemed to fit the skeptical spirit of the Enlightenment inasmuch as it enjoyed a vogue until 1820, the year of its last printing.

The turning point in Pascal scholarship came in 1842 when Victor Cousin, addressing the *Académie Française*, made an eloquent and dramatic plea for the establishment of a new text of the *Pensées* in accordance with a rigorous scrutiny of the original documents.

> What would one say if everyone knew that the original manuscript of Plato was in a public library and that, instead of having recourse to it and reforming the accepted text by the true one, the editors continued to copy from each other, without ever asking themselves if a phrase about which they were arguing, which some admired and which others censured, really belonged to Plato? But this is just what happens with the *Pensées* of Pascal. The autograph manuscript exists. It is at the Royal Library of Paris. Every editor speaks of it, none of them consults it, and the editions keep coming out. But take the trouble to go to the Rue Richelieu — it is not a long way — and you will be shocked at the enormous difference that the first glance will show you between the *pensées* of Pascal as they are written by his own hand, and as they are in all editions, without exception.[13]

Cousin then proceeded to point out the manifold defects of the Port-Royal edition. His chief counsels to future editors of the *Pensées* were, first, to establish an exact text by means of a comparison with the autographs, and second, to relegate to an appendix all of the *pensées* which were not written for the Apology.

It should be stressed at this point that the ensuing examination of the autographs did not shed any real light on the correct arrangement of the fragments. Gilberte Périer had kept Pascal's papers until her death in 1687 when they passed into the hands of her son Louis. In 1711 he had the fragments pasted onto stiff sheets of paper and bound in a volume so that, being of irregular size, they should not be lost or mislaid. This volume, known as the *Recueil Original*, is now ms. 9202 of the *fonds français* in the Bibliothèque Nationale (formerly the "Royal Library" mentioned by Cousin). It appears, however, that in the period from 1687 to 1711 Louis had deposited the papers in drawers at the library of Bienassis in Clermont, and that they were eventually pasted onto pages *in the order in which they were taken out of the drawers.* Moreover, it seems that whoever did the pasting was intent on filling up his pages as neatly and economically as possible. Thus he put as many fragments as he could on a page, sometimes snipping away their edges to make a fit possible.[14] Also, a few *pensées* must have been mislaid over the years since they appear in one or both of the Copies but not in the *Recueil Original*.

It is certainly true that the editions which followed Cousin's appeal (Faugère's, appearing in 1844, was the first) were an improvement on the old Port-Royal based editions inasmuch as they contained, not a selection, but all of the known *pensées* save for those few lost in the years before the *Recueil Original* was put together.

32

Still, there remained the problem of ordering the *pensées*, of finding a more or less clear line of argument in a seemingly inchoate mass of fragments. Most of the editions of the mid and late nineteenth century, e.g., those of Faugère (1844), Rocher (1893), Jeanin (1883) and Didiot (1896), purported to follow *"le plan de l'auteur,"* but in reality the plan was the editor's. In 1896 Gustave Michaut, rightly realizing the arbitrariness of these arrangements, presented the *Pensées* in the order of the *Recueil Original*, unaware that its order was not Pascal's either.[15] Needless to say, the lack of system in this arrangement had the additional drawback of perplexing the reader.

The most famous edition of the era was that of Léon Brunschvicg (1897, 1904). The work of an eminent educator, published by one of France's leading educational publishers (Librairie Hachette et C[ie.]), this edition acquired immense prestige. In fact, it still has many supporters in spite of its defects, largely on account of its excellent commentary and the coherence of its arrangement. Possibly reacting against the confusion of Michaut's arrangement, Brunschvicg presented the *Pensées* according to their *"continuité logique."* But unfortunately, his edition too distorted Pascal's thought. As Patricia Topliss points out:

> . . . the chief aim of Léon Brunschvicg was to make Pascal's thought as intelligible as possible to the general reader, and in order to achieve it he paid scant regard to such indications as we possess of the Apology's probable plan. The principal weaknesses of his edition are well known. By grouping the fragments on man's wretchedness and dispersing those on his greatness, Brunschvicg does much less than justice to the balance Pascal strives to maintain in his analysis of the duality of human nature; by distracting attention from his appeal to reason, he unduly emphasizes fideist tendencies; and in his effort to exhibit logical continuity in the fragments, he distorts his synthetic method.[16]

Since Brunschvicg's edition, the twentieth century has seen two major ways of grouping the *Pensées*.

The first is the arrangement into a coherent whole on the basis of reports of family or friends concerning Pascal's intentions for his Apology. This approach was followed in France by Jacques Chevalier (1925) and H. Massis (1930) and in England by H.F. Stewart (1942, 1950). The most influential source has been the *Discours sur les Pensées* of Filleau de la Chaise; Chevalier, Massis and Stewart all based their editions on his testimony. Filleau's account purports to be derived from an anonymous listener to a talk Pascal gave on his forthcoming Apology at Port-Royal in 1658. The reliability and completeness of Filleau's *Discours* and the feasibility of producing a truly Pascalian Apology from the indications it gives will be discussed in the next section of this chapter.

The second method eliminates the arbitrariness inherent in any reconstruction of Pascal's thought because it does not attempt one. This approach, by far the most sound, consists in publishing the *pensées* in the state in which they were left by Pascal. It gives us his partial classification of the fragments and to some extent his line of argument. Although they may not be what Pascal would have finally decided upon, they were nonetheless made definitive by his death. In short, this method obtrudes the minimun of editorial interference between Pascal and the reader.

Unfortunately, we are not *exactly* sure as to all of the details regarding the state of Pascal's papers at his death. It will be remembered that there are two Copies, each of which might be the one reflecting the precise order in which his papers were found. It is hardly surprising therefore that two editions, each claiming to reflect that order, compete for acceptance. Louis Lafuma, proceeding from the conjectures and intuitions of Zacharic Tourneur,[17] came to the conclusion that the First Copy (ms. 9203) was the one of which Étienne Périer spoke in his *Préface* and which reflected the order in which Pascal's papers were found. Thus, his more important editions (there are two types[18]) all reproduce the *Pensées* in the order of the First Copy (1951, 1958, 1962, 1963). The last of them appears in Pascal's *Oeuvres Complètes* in the *L'Intégrale* collection (Éditions du Seuil). It has become the standard edition of the *Pensées*. However, it has been recently challenged by the edition of Philippe Sellier (1976, Mercure de France) which presents the *Pensées* in the order of the Second Copy.

And so it is that the energy and assiduity of legions of editors over a span of more than three hundred years has finally succeeded in producing what may be regarded as the definitive edition of the *Pensées*, i.e., the one which presents the fragments in the order in which Pascal's family found them. Unfortunately, we do not know for certain just who has succeeded, the partisans of the First Copy or those of the Second.

Or is it unfortunate? My own view is that the claim of the Second Copy is much better,[19] but as a matter of fact I do not think that a great deal depends on the issue. It will be remembered that the order and contents of the *liasses à titres* and a Table of Contents are common to both Copies. To the student of Pascal's apologetics their interest far outweighs that of the sequence of the *liasses sans titres*, the chief point of difference between the two Copies. In fact Jean Mesnard, the *doyen* of Pascal scholars, has argued very persuasively that there is precious little order in the sequence of those *liasses* in either Copy.[20]

Consequently, let us begin our inquiry into the indications of Pascal's apologetic plan by examining what is certainly his work in the arrangement of the *pensées*[21] and should thus provide the necessary features of any future edition: the twenty-seven *liasses à titres* and the Table of Contents. We shall also examine testimony from Pascal's family and friends and procedural clues embedded in certain of the *pensées* themselves.

Internal and External Evidence for the Structure of Pascal's
Proposed Apology

Our evidence regarding the line of argument Pascal proposed to take in his Apology is of two kinds. The first consists of the Table of Contents and a few fragments on procedure to be found in the *Pensées* itself; the second, consisting of testimony of certain of his family and friends, is external to the *Pensées*.

Needless to say, there is no way of determining what the Apology would have been like had Pascal lived to complete it. Much ink has been spilled to little purpose on that topic. Indeed, if the Copies embody his very last efforts to order and classify his papers, then there is every reason to believe that he himself had not made the final determinations regarding the sequence and structure of his argument. We cannot say what he would have done, only what he intended to do. Therefore, our concern will be his apologetic plan *as reflected in* his papers and the testimony of his family and friends.

The state of his papers is partly described by the very important Table of Contents which appears three times in the two Copies.[22] It indicates the order in which the *liasses à titres* appear, which is as follows:

36

Order	A. P. R.
Vanity	Beginning
Wretchedness	Submission and Use of Reason
Boredom	Excellence
Sound Opinions of the People	Transition
Causes and Effects	Nature is Corrupt
Grandeur	Falseness of Other Religions
Contradictions	Religion is Lovable
Distraction	Foundations
Philosophers	Figurative Law
The Sovereign Good	Rabbinism
	Perpetuity
	Proofs of Moses
	Proofs of J. C.
	Prophecies
	Figures
	Christian Morality
	Conclusion

It should be noted that "Sound Opinions of the People" was crossed out by Pascal and a few *pensées* destined for it were incorporated into the *liasse* "Causes and Effects." Also, there is no *liasse* corresponding to the title "Nature is Corrupt." More important is the fact that some of the titles in the Table are abbreviated forms of those of the *liasses*. The more complete titles are: Boredom and Qualities Essential to Man; Submission and Use of Reason, in which True Christianity Consists; Excellence of this Way of Proving God; Transition from Knowledge of Man to Knowledge of God; Make Religion Lovable; Foundations of Religion and Response to Objections; That the Law was Figurative; and Particular Figures.

Now one of the most striking features of the Table is that the chapter headings are divided into two columns of unequal length, a fact which can hardly be accidental since it is found in all three specimens of the Table. But to what does this bipartite division correspond? This question is extremely important since its answer would yield the principal structural division envisaged by Pascal.

Fortunately, we have some fairly solid indications of its answer. They are to be found in *pensées* nos. six and twelve, in the *Préface* of Étienne Périer and in Filleau's *Discours*.

Here is number six:

First part: Wretchedness of man without God.
Second part: Happiness of man with God.
       otherwise
First part: Nature is corrupt, proved by nature itself.
Second part: There is a Redeemer, proved by Scripture.

This fragment has been extremely influential in scholars' assessments of the line of argument of the *Pensées*. A.J. Krailsheimer speaks for many when he says, prior to citing number six, that "The two poles of Pascal's argument are concisely defined at the beginning."[23] The information contained in six is most valuable, but as we shall see later it does not encompass Pascal's whole argument.

Nor does this fragment, although it too is most instructive.

Order. Men despise religion. They hate it and are afraid it may be true. The cure for this is first to show that religion is not contrary to reason, but worthy of reverence and respect.

Next make it appear attractive, make good men wish it were true, and then show that it is.

Worthy of reverence because it has really understood human nature.

Attractive because it promises true good. (#12)

38

I would like to postpone a consideration of these two *pensées*[24] until the testimony of family and friends has been seen. Even so, we may note here that the first fragment structures the argument with reference to man while the second does so with reference to religion. But more of this anon.

The main external evidence regarding Pascal's apologetic plan is to be found in Étienne Périer's *Préface,* Filleau's *Discours,* Gilberte Périer's *Vie de M. Pascal* and Pierre Nicole's *Traité de l'éducation d'un prince.*[25]

The accounts of Gilberte and Nicole are very cursory and quite incomplete. Nonetheless, both forcefully make the point that Pascal did not intend to avail himself of metaphysical proof and proofs from nature.[26] He respected such arguments but did not think them within the grasp of very many; hence he did not value them for apologetics. If nothing else, this shows us the kind of audience for which the Apology was destined — *libertins* and *honnêtes gens*, hardened skeptics of a worldly bent, not a small circle of metaphysically minded savants.

The productions of Étienne and Filleau are much more important, this despite the latter's diffuseness and prolixity. They too are incomplete, as are all of our evidences regarding Pascal's intentions, but at least they are in fundamental agreement. This is not surprising considering that Étienne had Filleau's *Discours* at hand when he was composing his own work. Both of course had access to at least the First Copy, and both claimed to derive information second-hand from a talk Pascal once gave on his apologetic project at Port-Royal.[27]

Étienne and Filleau both affirm that Pascal will begin with a portrayal of the human condition in its internal and external aspects.[28] The purpose of this *peinture de l'homme* is to lead the unbeliever to a kind of self-knowledge that will shock and disturb him. In particular, Pascal will dwell on the duality of human nature, its greatness and wretchedness, its strengths and frailties. It is hoped that the unbeliever will be stimulated to enquire into the reasons for the manifold contrarieties his nature displays. Why is man as he is? What are his origins? And what fate awaits this peculiar creature after death? Once these questions are seriously posed they will demand an answer. But where are answers to be found?

First the philosophers will be examined. Perhaps truth resides with them. But, alas, their jarring doctrines are riddled with errors, a fact which is in large part a consequence of the weakness of the rational faculty.

But what about religions? There has been "an infinity" of them throughout the ages, but, as Filleau points out,[29] some begin with a certain people and end with them; some are not in the least spiritual or elevated but authorize vice or worship gods worse than men; and some have been established by force, others by chicanery. Passing from these, at last the unbeliever's gaze will come to a certain people which is most ancient and remarkable, the Jews. They have all sprung from one man, and they have shown an extraordinary reluctance to being assimilated by other nations. And they have a book which is unique in that it contains their laws, history and religion. What does it say?

At this point the unbeliever is told the story of salvation history as recounted in the Old and New Testaments. Although the "proofs"[30] of Christianity have not yet been presented to him, he should still find the Biblical account most intriguing and impressive. Specifically, he should find it worthy of belief because it speaks of Deity in a fitting manner. It also explains his curious dual nature and provides a remedy for it, and as Filleau notes[31] it does the same for the puzzling hiddenness of God. Moreover, it alone among religions has preached a gospel of love. For all of these reasons the unbeliever should come to wish that Christianity might be true, and this will put him in the proper frame of mind to consider its "proofs."

Filleau and Étienne both agree that the first of the actual "proofs" of Christianity was to be the evidence of Moses.[32] In particular, Pascal meant to call attention to the miracles of Moses, performed in the sight of hundreds of thousands, the figurative character of the Mosaic Law and his prophecies of Christ's birth. These considerations, found in a book which we have every reason to trust,[33] are strong indeed when we add to them Christ's birth and life, which fulfilled the prophecies, his miracles and the sublime character of his doctrine. And we can be sure that the Apostles, who first spread the news of his life and doctrine, transmitted them faithfully. Not to have done so would have meant that they were either fools or scoundrels, both of which hypotheses are untenable.

Such in brief are the main lines of Pascal's apologetic argument as represented by Étienne and Filleau. Although their information is far from unhelpful, it is not altogether satisfactory as an exposition of Pascal. For one thing, although their account is in rough accord with the Table of Contents it is hard to square the two exactly. For example, in Étienne and Filleau the examination of the religions directly follows that of the philosophers whereas in the Table "Falseness of Other Religions" is the eighth title after "Philosophers." One could, I suppose, argue that the order of the Table here is so unsatisfactory that it is no wonder that neither Étienne nor Filleau adhered to it. More troubling by far, however, are their omissions. Like Gilberte and Nicole, neither mentions the wager argument, nowadays the most famous element of the Pascalian corpus. This is all the more unfortunate considering that the wager is found in the *liasses sans titres*. Where would it have figured in the Apology? What role would it have played? Since neither Pascal nor any of his circle tells us,[34] these things must be inferred from an analysis of the wager itself and of the Apology's over-all *continuité logique*. My own views on the role of the wager will be found in the next section of this chapter.

Other prominent themes in the *Pensées* also go unmentioned in the summaries of Étienne and Filleau, notably distraction and perpetuity. But since distraction is obviously a part of the *peinture de l'homme* and perpetuity is a "proof" founded on Scripture, their absence is far less vexing than that of the wager.

But despite the shortcomings of their accounts, Étienne and Filleau tell us much about the general structure of Pascal's argument. Both agree that the "proofs" of Christianity were to come at the end, and that the part containing the "proofs" was to be preceded by a long attempt to put the unbeliever in the right frame of mind to take them seriously. In other words, they agree that the Apology was to be divided into a persuasive part containing an analysis of the human condition and a probative one consisting of "proofs" from the Scriptures. What light does this shed on the evidence of the Table and of *pensées* six and twelve? And what can we now say about the over-all structure of Pascal's argument?

Let us consider the following points:

1) The division of the Apology into persuasive and probative parts implicit in Filleau and Étienne is very reasonable in itself, but Pascal nowhere sets forth this division explicitly. Moreover, it does not harmonize exactly with his own division in the Table since the "proofs" take up only the last part of column two.

2) Fragment six does not harmonize exactly with the Table either although it comes nearer to doing so. The first division of six ("misery of man without God") accords well with column one inasmuch as "The Sovereign Good" closes the critique of the philosophers for the present. In column one many questions are raised to vex the unbeliever but he is offered no enlightenment or consolation. Column two, with its examination of religions, does offer enlightenment and consolation. Insofar as it does so it illustrates "the happiness of man with God," the second division of fragment six. But column two also contains the "proofs" and so it is more inclusive than the second division of six.

3) Fragment twelve is also less inclusive than the Table. Twelve would a) make men reverence and respect religion as not contrary to reason, b) make them wish that it were true, and c) show them that it is true. This division agrees well with the order of the *liasses* in column two, but it does not extend to column one.

4) Examined by themselves, columns one and two of the Table seem to correspond to a portrayal of the human condition and an examination of religion, respectively. The examination of religion seems to consist roughly of two parts. The first might be called "Transition from the Knowledge of Man to the Knowledge of God." It would show that the questions regarding man's origin, nature and fate raised earlier can be answered fittingly and beautifully by Christianity alone among religions. It would make one wish that it might be true. The second part of course consists of the "proofs."

On the basis of these points, I think that we may fairly draw the following conclusions:

1) There is an over-lap in the divisions of fragments six and twelve. When one has been brought to wish that Christianity might be true so that his doubts might be allayed, his woes consoled and his deficiencies remedied, he has been shown the "happiness of man with God."

2) Neither six nor twelve is as broad in scope as the Table of Contents. Since both of them omit part of the argument the divisions of the Table are preferable to theirs.

3) The divisions of the Table should also take precedence over the useful persuasive/probative dichotomy implicit in Étienne and Filleau. The Table is after all Pascal's own work.

4) The *liasses* designated in column one of the Table contain material for a portrayal of the human condition; those in column two for an examination of religion. Column two also contains prefatory or transitional material.

With these conclusions in mind, we may represent the structure of Pascal's apologetic argument as follows. Note that the divisions derived from Filleau and Étienne are set off by broken lines.

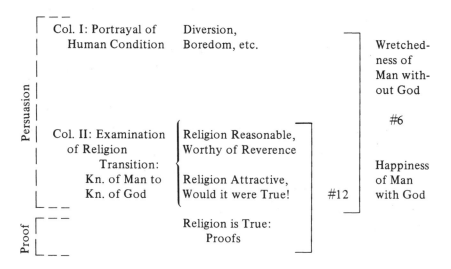

44

I take the schema above to display the main lines of Pascal's Apology as reflected in his *pensées* and in the testimony of his circle. The schema supplements the informative accounts of Étienne and Filleau in that it shows us, not just a sequence of arguments, but an arrangement of the themes which the arguments are meant to illustrate. An appreciation of both is needful if one is to arrive at a thorough understanding of Pascal's case for Christianity.

Now that we know something of the structure and direction of his apologetic argument, and now that we have a salutary notion of the difficulties attendant on any attempt to see it as a coherent whole, let us consider its principal steps in some detail.

Pascal's Apology for the Christian Religion

I The Human Condition

Pascal thought he could show that a man, not a believer but rational and of good faith, could be brought to see the reasonableness of Christianity and to embrace it by argumentation quite as cogent as that which men are wont to accept in other matters. The account which follows presents his Apology as I think it was meant to proceed. Needless to say, in point of fact the audience may not be as docile as I have represented it or as Pascal hoped.

He meant to begin with a portrait of the human condition that would give rise to a variety of disturbing questions. Pascal affirms that even the most cursory inspection of man will reveal that he is a mass of contradictions. He is wretched, "vile enough to bow down to the beasts and worship them" (#53). And he is great: "It is not in space that I must seek my human dignity, but in the ordering of my thought. . . . Through space the universe comprehends me and swallows me up like a speck; through thought I comprehend it" (#113). And he is strong, this "supreme judge of the world," yet weak:

> It does not take a cannon's roar to arrest his thoughts; the noise of a weathercock or pulley will do. Do not be surprised if his reasoning is not too sound at the moment, there is fly buzzing round his ears. . . . If you want him to be able to find the truth, drive away the creature that is paralysing his reason and disturbing the mighty intelligence that rules over cities and kingdoms. (#48)

What can we say of this creature who alone among animals has reason but is so often ruled instead by his imagination?[35] How could such a collection of contraries have come to be in the first place? What is his true nature? Must he live always at the level of his nature or may he hope to remedy its defects? And what destiny awaits him after death?

The usual procedure for avoiding an encounter with such troubling questions is simply to ignore them and to focus attention instead on the ephemeral banalities of existence. This shift of focus away from matters of the utmost consequence for us to others of little moment Pascal calls "distraction."[36]

> H5. When I see the blind and wretched state of man, when I survey the whole universe in its dumbness and man left to himself with no light, as though lost in this corner of the universe, without knowing who put him there, what he has come to do, what will become of him when he

dies, incapable of knowing anything, I am moved to terror. . . . Then I marvel that so wretched a state does not drive people to despair. I see other people around me, made like myself. I ask them if they are any better informed than I, and they say they are not. Then these lost and wretched creatures look around and find some attractive objects to which they become addicted and attached. For my part, I have never been able to form such attachments. . . .[37]   (#198)

Distraction. Being unable to cure death, wretchedness and ignorance, men have decided, in order to be happy, not to think about such things.
        (#133)

But once men become conscious of the fact that they are distracting themselves the spell of distraction is broken. Pascal hopes they will become acutely conscious of a need to learn what truth they can about themselves and their fate. Indifference to the ultimate questions should be out of the question[38] since no one wants to be made miserable by ignorance and doubt, and distraction, having been exposed, is no longer likely to be very efficacious in alleviating them. In short, the unbelievers' happiness, which had hitherto rested on distraction,[39] is now undone and the new ignorance of their true condition leaves them feeling wretched and alone.[40] They are condemned therefore to seek such truth as they can find. But where shall they enquire?

First they may ask among the philosophers. Of course the skeptics in the philosophical crowd will not be of any help; they maintain that nothing is known or even that to say "nothing is known" is to say too much. But the "dogmatic" philosophers not only admit the possiblility of knowledge but claim to have it. Each of these sages has a teaching on human nature, right rules of conduct, the immortality of the soul and so on. Perhaps one or more of them can dispel the cloud of unknowing in which the unbelievers grope.

Unfortunately, there is not even rough agreement among these divine minds as to what the truth of the most important matters is. *Quot homines, tot sententiae.* And worse yet, their teaching are vulnerable to the misologic attacks of the skeptics.

Although not a skeptic himself,[41] Pascal, following Montaigne, sides with them insofar as he realizes that reason cannot defend itself against their assaults. Pascal's chief criticism of reason concerns its *scope*. On his view there are kinds of things which reason is simply unable to encompass. If we are to know them, another faculty must serve.

> We know the truth not only through our reason but also through our heart. It is through the latter that we know first principles, and reason, which has nothing to do with this process, tries in vain to refute them . . . . We know that we are not dreaming, but, however unable we may be to prove it rationally, our inability proves nothing but the weakness of our reason, and not the uncertainty of our knowledge. . . . Principles are felt, propositions proved, and both with certainty though by different means.[42]   (#110)

Nor is reason on very sure ground even within its own domain. There is an enemy in the house, and the result is civil war.

> Man is nothing but a subject full of natural error. . . . Nothing shows him the truth, everything deceives him. The two principles of truth, reason and the senses, are not only both not genuine, but are engaged in mutual deception. The senses deceive reason through false appearances, and, just as they trick the soul, they are tricked by it in their turn: it takes its revenge. The senses are disturbed by passions, which produce false impressions. They both compete in lies and deception.
> (#45)

From these considerations it follows that, despite the claims of some philosophers, they have no trustworthy answers to the most important questions about human life and death. Their doctrines are a product of their reason, a faculty which cannot apprehend first principles and which is subject to all sorts of error even when operating within its proper sphere. Who would be so rash as to decide the most momentous questions on the basis of notions arrived at through so suspect an instrument?

Where else then might the unbelievers inquire?

What of the world's religions? They, like the greater part of the philosophers, claim to know what man is, whence he is sprung, how he should live and what will befall him after death. Should not their doctrines be scrutinized?

But wait. The wisdom of the philosophers was discredited by showing its source, reason, to be limited and untrustworthy. But what of the source or ground of religious teachings? They are said to derive from Divinity. Now the unbelievers cannot be expected to give credence to any of these teachings unless they believe that there *is* such a thing as Divinity. Unless one is prepared to grant that there is a *theos* to give a *logos* of, one has no reason to take any theological account seriously. And this of course is precisely what the unbeliever, just because he is an unbeliever, is not prepared to grant.[43] Since he does not believe in Divinity, why should he lend credence to anything which purports to be an account of or revelation from the Divine? In short, why grant *any* religion a serious hearing?

II Religion: Transition from Knowledge of Man to Knowledge of God

The preceding question is one which the wager can answer. It seems that Pascal meant it to show, not that one should believe in the *Christian* God, but that one ought to believe in *a* God who has a plan for men which includes an afterlife.[44]

The wager, found in the fragment *"Infini-rien"* (#418), is not a metaphysical argument for God's existence. The frailties of reason aside, such arguments suffer from a decided want of rhetorical force: an hour after assenting one wonders if perhaps it was not all dialectical sleight-of-hand. The wager appeals to prudence and self-interest, considerations which most men find weightier by far than metaphysics. And, as the following summary of the argument indicates, it does not aim to prove that a God of a certain kind actually exists; it only means to show that we ought to *believe* that he does and live accordingly.

Is there a God or is there not? We cannot know for certain, says Pascal, but a reasonable man will soon see that he ought to wager that there is. If your chances of winning a bet are fifty-fifty and you stand to lose as much as you stand to gain, then the choice of whether or not to bet is one of indifference. But if you stand to win twice as much as you stand to lose, i.e., if the odds are two to one, then you would be a fool not to bet. Now if God exists and you have "bet" on his existence by believing in him and living accordingly, you stand to gain an eternity of felicity.[45] In other words, one who wagers on God's existence stakes one lifetime of belief and conduct but stands to win an infinite number of happy lives (an eternity of felicity). Since the chances of

God's existing are fifty-fifty (or at least not infinitely small), you must have renounced reason not to have bet that God exists.

This argument has drawn heavy criticism over the years though by no means is all of that criticism sound.[46] In fact, if one keeps in mind the limited role the wager is meant to play, it is not clear that any of the traditional criticisms are really damaging. But this much at least is certain: if the argument is successful, Pascal will have brought unbelievers to believe, even if only grudgingly *at first*.[47] Genuine faith may come later. Also, it is of the utmost importance to note that it is not merely on a God that one is to wager but on a God of Judgment. The God of the wager is committed to rewarding his faithful with bliss eternal and, at the least, withholding it from others. Such a deity is not far removed from the Apology's *terminus ad quem*, the God of Abraham, Isaac and Jacob.

Once an unbeliever has made the wager he must admit that some religion *could* be true since, after all, he is committed to belief in a Deity. And since the wager has induced him to believe also that this Deity will reward some and not others, the unbeliever will have good reason for thinking that he must have made his will known to men. If the God of the wager were not to have done this he would be monstrously unjust, an attribute scarcely compatible with divinity. But to say all of this — that one believes in a God who, by inference,[48] must have made his will known to men — means that one has very good grounds for believing that at least one religion, at least one supposed divine revelation, is genuine.

Let us therefore scrutinize the various religions. Is it credible that any of them is of divine origin? Do any seem to possess the truths for which the unbelievers have sought thus far in vain?

Alas, they present a sorry spectacle indeed! The "Falsity of Other Religions," as Pascal's chapter heading has it, should be all too evident to the careful enquirer. As a matter of fact, the only religion besides Christianity which Pascal brings forward for much consideration is Islam. (He does of course treat Judaism at some length, but he assimilates it into the Christian scheme of things with the standard assertion that the Jewish Scriptures prove Jesus.) Against Islam he notes that Mahomet was not foretold and that he slew.[49] If we may trust Filleau (pp. CCVI— CCVII), Pascal would have had a good deal more to say about the falseness of other religions and would have included more on other faiths, such as those of China.

Finally, Pascal would have the unbelievers cast their eyes on a singular people possessed of a singular book. This people, the Jews, all sprung from one man, most ancient yet continuing unto our own days, has texts which contain its history, law and religion. What do they say? What light have they?

Now the unbelievers will be told the Christian world-story, rooted as it is in the books of the Jews. They will hear of the Creation and of the Fall and its calamitous results: the corruption of human nature and the estrangement of God from man. They will learn how this God parted the veil of his hiddenness for a time in the Incarnation, and how grace was made available to redeem men from sin. And they will be told of the Resurrection with its promise of eternal life.

Although this story is as yet unproved, there should exist in the unbelievers a strong presumption in its favor.

First of all, it alone speaks worthily of the divine, Pascal would say. Unlike the fables of other sects, it does not speak of Divinity and life to come in gross and carnal terms, nor does it impute to God aught unfitting.

Secondly, it acquires much additional verisimilitude from the fact that it accounts for what (little) we can know of God and human nature from the world about us.

Now that man's nature is dual, says Pascal, is the most obvious of verities.[50]

> Is it not clear as day that man's condition is dual? The point is that if man had never been corrupted, he would, in his innocence, confidently enjoy both truth and felicity, and, if man had never been anything but corrupt, he would have no idea either of truth or of bliss.
> (#131)

It follows then that the religion which teaches the true nature of the relationship of man to God will be one which proclaims man's dual nature.

> Man's greatness and wretchedness are so evident that the true religion must necessarily teach us that there is in man some great principle of greatness and some great principle of wretchedness.
> It must also account for such amazing contradictions.
>
> . . . .
>
> It must teach us the cure for our helplessness and the means of obtaining this cure. Let us examine all the religions of the world on that point and let us see whether any but the Christian religion meets it.
> (#149)

In point of fact, Pascal says, no religion but Christianity does meet these conditions. It teaches that man's nature is dual; it accounts for this via the doctrine of the Fall; it proclaims the remedy, grace, made accessible through the Redemption; and it tells how this grace is bestowed.

53

But what of God? What do we know of him by our natural light? Clearly, one can search nature up and down and find no unambiguous trace of him.[51] It is obvious, then, that any God must be a Hidden God, and that no religion which fails to proclaim one can be true.

Now Christianity not only preaches a Hidden God but explains why he has not chosen to reveal himself unambiguously.

> If he wished to overcome the obstinacy of the most hardened, he could have done so by revealing himself to them so plainly that they could not doubt the truth of his essence, as he will appear on the last day with such thunder and lightning and such convulsions of nature that the dead will rise up and the blindest will see him. This is not the way he wished to appear when he came in mildness, because so many men had shown themselves unworthy of his clemency, that he wished to deprive them of the good they did not desire . . . but neither was it right that his coming should be so hidden that he could not be recognized by those who sincerely sought him. He wished to make himself perfectly recognizable to them. Thus . . . he has qualified our knowledge of him by giving signs which can be seen by those who seek him and not by those who do not.[52]   (#149)

In addition to recognizing and explaining God's hiddenness, Christianity offers those who seek him a means of overcoming it somewhat. It is Jesus Christ, the same remedy offered for the ills of man's corruption. Through the Redemption he brings pardon for transgression and through his own dual nature, divine and human, he provides a bridge between God and man. Through him the Hidden God is in a manner revealed. Without this revelation we would grope in almost utter ignorance.

The third consideration which is to predispose the unbelievers in Christianity's favor is the heart-felt wish that it might be true.

How could they not desire this? For if what they have heard is so, then the doubts and uncertainties which vex them can at last be allayed, the remedy for their ills is at hand and they have the prospect of attaining true and abiding good, bliss eternal. Would then that it were true!

From a rhetorical point of view, this is the crucial step in the Apology. A man can consider any possibility or probability without being in the least emotionally touched by it. If he is to be brought to belief, it is best to capture his will first. Like imagination, the will is quite capable of leading reason "by its nose," as it were. It too is a *puissance trompeuse*.

> The will is one of the chief organs of belief, not because it creates belief, but because things are true or false according to the aspect by which we judge them. When the will likes one aspect more than another, it deflects the mind from considering the qualities it does not care to see. (#539)

Another facet of the will's role is its propensity to find fault in things which it does not like, e.g., in what is frightening. Hence Pascal's "scare tactics," his soul-wrenching portrayal of man's misery and isolation without God and his likening of the human condition to that of captives in a dungeon awaiting execution.

Pascal did not mean to sow seed amid rocks and thorns if he could help it. Now at least his audience should be in the proper frame of mind to receive the "proofs" of the Christian faith.

III Religion: "Proofs"

According to Pascal, the truth of Christianity is established by the signs of divine sanction and approbation which foreshadowed it and which have ever accompanied it, albeit in decreasing numbers. Chief among these signs are miracles and prophecies.

It is imperative to keep in mind that these signs are not proof in the sense that demonstations *more geometrico* are. One can refuse to believe in miracles without renouncing reason.

> The prophecies, even the miracles and proofs of our religion, are not of such a kind that they can be said to be absolutely convincing, but they are at the same time such that it cannot be said to be unreasonable to believe in them. . . . But the evidence [in their favor] is such as to exceed, or at least equal, evidence to the contrary, so that it cannot be reason that decides against us following it, and can therefore only be concupiscence and wickedness of heart.   (#835)

Pascal holds miracles to be the chief of Christianity's "proofs."[53] "Jesus proved he was the Messiah, but never by proving his doctrine from the Scripture or the prophecies, but always by miracles" (#846). Thus, "It would have been no sin not to have believed in Jesus Christ without miracles" (#184). But why then should the men of today, none or very few of whom see miracles, believe in him? Pascal's answer is that miracles were necessary in Christ's time but no longer are required. Today, the fulfillment of the prophecies suffices.

> Jesus Christ performed miracles, and then the apostles, and the early saints in great numbers, because, since the prophecies were not yet

fulfilled, and were being fulfilled by them, there was no witness save
that of miracles. . . . Now there is no more need of miracles against the
Jews, for the fulfillment of the prophecies is a continuing miracle.
(#180)

Pascal realizes that there are problems with his position on the
importance of miracles. How do we know that there have ever
been any miracles? And since other faiths may claim their support
as well, should they not be considered to have been proved?

His response to the first question is a bit strained:

> . . . the reason we believe in so many false effects of the moon is that
> there are some genuine ones, like the tides of the seas. It is the same with
> miracles, prophecies, divination by dreams, spells, etc., for if none of
> this had ever been genuine, none of it would ever have been believed.
> Thus, instead of concluding that there are no true miracles because
> there are so many false ones, we must on the contrary say that there
> certainly are true miracles since there are so many false ones. . . .[54]
> (#743)

But what about miracles attested by other faiths? Pascal replies
that, just as miracles prove doctrine, so doctrine proves miracles:
God would not let miracles be performed on behalf of doctrines
not manifestly false.

Now, it sounds patently circular to say that miracles prove
doctrine and vice-versa. Pascal, however, seems to put a bit more
emphasis on miracles proving doctrine (#841). If miracles seem to
have been performed on behalf of doctrines not manifestly false or
antecedently pronounced suspect by reliable sources, this should
be sufficient. The truth will be there and within our grasp, for
Pascal — like Descartes — affirms that God is not a deceiver.

57

Men owe it to God to accept the religion he sends them.

God owes it to men not to lead them into error.

Now, they would be led into error if the workers of miracles proclaimed a doctrine not visibly false in the light of common sense, and if a greater worker of miracles had not already warned them not to believe such men.

. . . .

There is therefore no difficulty when miracles and a doctrine above suspicion are found together on the same side, but when miracles and a suspect doctrine are found on the same side, we must then see which is the clearer. (#840)

There is no difficulty, however, in the case of Christianity. When one considers the wonders performed on its behalf in conjunction with its sublime morality, there is no reason to hesitate. Indeed, Pascal considers Christian morality itself to be a "proof" (nos. 402, 482).

Aside from miracles, the principal signs of Christianity's truth are the prophecies and perpetuity.

Pascal finds a powerful argument in the fulfillment of the prophecies.

If a single man had written a book foretelling the time and manner of Jesus's coming and Jesus had come in conformity with these prophecies, this would carry infinite weight.

But there is much more here. There is a succession of men over a period of 4,000 years, coming consistently and invariably one after the other, to foretell the same coming; there is an entire people proclaiming it, existing for 4,000 years to testify in a body to the certainty they feel about it, from which they cannot be deflected by whatever threats and persecutions they may suffer. This is of quite a different order of importance. (#332)

But even the prophecies, owing to their figurative character, are not unambiguous signs. Like the other "proofs" they are such as to convince only those who genuinely seek; the hard of heart they will not persuade (#255).

The key to the figures, says Pascal, lies in the nature of the goods foretold by the prophets. The material goods spoken of were actually meant as a figure for spiritual goods. On this view, the carnal among the Jews took the prophecies at face value, expected material benefits (e.g., an earthly "Kingdom of God"), and thus rejected the Messiah because he did not bring them. But others among the Jews, expecting spiritual things, hailed the works of Jesus as the fulfillment of the prophecies.

Moreover, this split among the Jews yields yet another sign of Christianity's truth, for it renders them more credible witnesses of Jesus. "If the Jews had all been converted by Christ, we should have only suspect witnesses left" (#592). Furthermore, "by killing him and continuing to deny him they fulfilled the prophecies" (#487).

And so one should see that the prophecies truly foretold Christ's coming, and did it in the way characteristic of God in his dealings with men. Only enough light is provided for those who yearn to find him to see; the hard of heart will not see.

Yet another "proof" of Christianity is perpetuity. In one form or another it has existed always, from the first man, Adam, to the last, those of the present. "The Messiah has always been believed in" (#282). This is even more striking and marvelous when one considers how unnatural Christianity is. For example, it is hostile to the ego insofar as it teaches that one must renounce one's own will for God's (*fiat voluntas tua*), and it has rather circumscribed ideas about what is licit in the domain of sensual pleasure (#284).

Of course, the antiquity of a belief as such does not hallow or prove it. Presumably Pascal felt that, since it is reasonable to suppose that God has always been concerned with men, the original religion is the genuine one. And perhaps he felt that Christianity's long survival and its rapid spread despite persecution and its unnaturalness bespoke the efforts of some Providence on its behalf.

Although these "proofs" are not of such a kind as to coerce assent, nonetheless Pascal hoped that they would persuade unbelievers whose hearts he had tried to incline towards Christ earlier in the Apology. Having seen that Christianity is attractive and worthy of belief, they have now been shown evidence for it which is as solid as one can rightly expect.

It is obvious that the probative power of Christianity's miracles, prophecies and perpetuity depends on the Bible's veracity and on the correctness of interpreting its narrative as figurative in some parts and literally true in others. If, as seems certain, skeptics were to crave some assurance of its underlying veracity and of the fitness of Pascal's exegetical technique, what would he say?

We know that Pascal meant to speak against the excessive use of figures in Biblical interpretation (#254), but he did not do so in the *Pensées*. It is not clear, therefore, just how he would have responded to an assertion that the bulk of the Scriptural narrative, including the accounts of the Incarnation, Resurrection, miracles, etc., was not to be taken *ad litteram* but *sensu allegorico*. Perhaps he would have countered that a figurative interpretation is permissible only if Scripture itself tells us that figures are meant, as is the case with the parables and with the prophets (see Hosea, 12:10), or if there is no other way of interpreting the passages in question reasonably.

Pascal does sketch several arguments for the general trustworthiness of the Scripture. He took the long lives of the patriarchs and the consequent fewness of generations across long expanses of time as an indication of the reliability of the Old Testament accounts. Even though Moses lived a very long time after the Flood, he would not be separated by so very many generations from Noah, and so the traditions of the Deluge would still be distinct in Moses's time.[55] Moreover, the Jews have always been most painstaking and scrupulous with regard to their history; this too should be taken into account.

As for the New Testament, Pascal considers the truth of its central doctrine, the Resurrection, to be evidenced by the reliability of the Apostles as witnesses (#310). The argument, with a few steps filled in, is as follows: Either the Apostles told the truth about Christ's Resurrection or they spoke falsely. If they spoke falsely, they did so knowingly or unknowingly. If knowingly, they were knaves; if unknowingly, dupes. But how could they have been mistaken in thinking that Christ had appeared to them several times after his death? They could not have been dupes. And what save ridicule and persecution had they to gain by concocting a wild story about a man rising from the dead? Knaves do not seek such "gain," so they could not have been knaves. Since they were neither knaves nor dupes, it is not the case that they spoke falsely; they said what was. Pascal might well continue that once the truth of the Resurrection has been granted there is little reason to baulk at crediting the rest of the New Testament. If Christ rose he is God. Whence then the difficulty?

And so in sum the book grounding the "proofs" is one we have reason to believe to be trustworthy and true. This ground is like the "proofs" themselves — solid but not unshakable. And so the "proofs" stand, and with them the argument of the Apology.

Such are the principal lines of Pascal's apologetic argument as it has come down to us. Even though what we have is not a finished product but a work "frozen" at an earlier or later point in its development, it exhibits considerable coherence and strength. In essence, what Pascal does is to wage a war of attrition against unbelief. He puts forth a variety of themes and arguments, no one of which is decisive either logically or rhetorically, but which — after many *entrecroisements* and *reprises* — coalesce into a powerful challenge to unbelief. His is a serious attempt to show the attractiveness and reasonableness of a doctrine which, as he himself admits, cannot be conclusively established by anything short of the lightnings of the last day.

It need hardly be said that Pascal's arguments have met with many objections. A few have already been mentioned in the text and notes, namely those pertaining to the wager, to the authenticity of at least some miracles, and to the reliability of the Old Testament from the long lives of the patriarchs. Although my object has been to offer an exposition rather than a critique of his apologetics, some additional critical remarks are still in order.

From a rhetorical point of view, the Apology's success is by no means assured despite Pascal's best efforts at exploiting the intricacies of a very sophisticated *art de persuader*. Pascal has shown that indifference to the ultimate questions *ought* to be out of the question, that the *libertin ought* to feel miserable in the idle pusuit of *divertissement*, but this does not mean that it *will* be so. The gap between "is" and "ought" cannot be bridged by the apologist alone, and the reader need not cooperate with him. The willingness to pursue the search along Pascal's lines cannot be extorted from him by main dialectical force.

The extent to which Pascal has (perhaps inevitably) failed in this regard is apparent from the reasons behind the *Pensées'* enduring popularity. It has succeeded, not as a proselytizing tool, but as great literature. It is most often read, not by eventual converts, but by admirers of his insight into human nature and of the haunting beauty of his expression. It is esteemed, not as an Apology, but as a compendium of brilliant aphorisms. In the *Pensées*, Pascal has succeeded *malgré lui*.

From a philosophical point of view, one may raise objections to some of Pascal's most basic assumptions. In particular:

— Pascal assumes that the Bible is to be understood *ad litteram* in some contexts and in an allegorical way reminiscent of Philo Judaeus in others. But both ways, as used by Pascal, would be difficult to defend in the light of contemporary Biblical criticism. It has a strong current of demythologizing which will not allow the texts to be taken as plain history, and it has long since discarded the notion of the Bible as a sort of *roman à clef* sent from on high to exercise the allegorically-inclined exegete.

This is a very strong objection, but it need not be fatal to Pascal's over-all argument. Without entering into an appraisal of the soundness of contemporary Biblical interpretation, one may point out that Pascal's argument requires only a coherent exegetical method which would preserve the historicity of at least some miracles, e.g., the Resurrection, and allow for the fulfillment of prophecies. The method in question need not be Pascal's.

— Pascal's skepticism is a two edged sword. It undercuts the apologist as well as the philosopher. If reason is so frail, so restricted and so liable to error, why should the apologist's arguments be trusted any more than those of the philosophers? Of course Pascal would answer that *"soumission de la raison"* is far from utter disparagement of it, but there is a fine line between humbling reason and hamstringing it, so to speak. Is our reason sound enough to inform us correctly when reason should submit? Pascal concedes enough to the skeptics to make one uneasy on this score.

— Pascal holds the sublimity of Christian morality to be one of his faith's "proofs." But theoretical and practical objections to Christian morality can certainly be raised.

Nietzsche, as we shall see, provides us with prize specimens of the former while Christians have obligingly provided us with myriad specimens of the latter. Pascal did not see fit to mention the Portuguese and Spanish *autos da fe*, the condemnation of his fellow physicist Galileo, and of course the bloody *nuit de Saint-Barthélemy* (August 23, 1572). "By their fruits ye shall know them," a facetious *libertin* might say. And needless to say, the few events noted above are far from exhausting the catalogue of iniquities which have been committed, not only by Christians, but "for the faith" and with Church approval at one level or another.

— The argument of perpetuity is founded on what seems to be an empirically false premise, viz., that the Jewish faith, stretching back to Adam, is of greater antiquity than any other. This argument cannot be salvaged, but it is not indispensable.

— His analysis of rival religions is quite inadequate although, if we may believe Filleau, he would have added to it considerably. Short shrift to other religions may have been dictated by the make-up of Pascal's intended audience as well as by the impoverished state of the study of comparative religions in his day. Hinduism and Buddhism can hardly have been "live options" to the *libertins* and *honnêtes gens*.

This is a serious drawback because the case for Christianity, though strong, is inconclusive. One might well wonder if some other faith did not have an even stronger case. Perhaps Pascal would reply that God could not allow a false faith to appear so firmly supported without failing in his duty not to mislead men.

As a matter of fact, Pascal himself makes up one of the chorus of his Apology's critics, although his reservation is of a different sort from those voiced above. He laments that the most he can do is to induce the reader to give intellectual assent to certain propositions embodying truths of the faith. This intellectual assent is not faith, which is the knowing of God through the heart. Only God can give this, and without it there is no salvation (nos. 808, 110). In other words, apologetics, unable to achieve its true end unaided, is in itself a vain endeavor. Thus, as M. and M.R. Le Guern remark, the *Pensées* "is not the cry of joy of a man who has found the truth and wishes to share his certitude; it is the tragic cry of one who knows where the truth is, who does all that he can so that it might be recognized, but does not hide from himself the profound vanity of his attempt to do so."[56]

Now we turn to another member of the chorus, a thinker who reacted very strongly indeed to Pascal and Christianity, a man who loved Pascal and yet was his antipode in many respects — Friedrich Nietzsche.

CHAPTER TWO

NIETZSCHE CONTRA THE CRUCIFIED

Like Pascal, Nietzsche left behind him a great mass of fragments and drafts, his *Nachlass*, and an unfinished work dealing with Christianity. Of his projected four-part Revaluation of all Values only *The Antichrist* was completed before the crepuscular curtain of madness descended on him in January, 1889. But happily, it is not necessary to piece together Nietzsche's position on Christianity from the *Nachlass*. His fragments and drafts are interesting in their own right and they shed light on the genesis of his published works. Still, the all-but-illegibility of much of this material, the fact that much in it is undoubtedly provisional or experimental and the fact that Nietzsche chose not to publish it count strongly against relying heavily on it. Moreover, a man who writes fourteen books has not left himself without witness; there is no need to rummage through his dustbin and old notebooks to discover what he thought. What is best in Nietzsche is to be found, as he himself insisted (EH III), in his books.

The estimate of the *Nachlass* applies also to biographical considerations — they too have a real but decidedly limited importance in the study of Nietzsche. They do indeed furnish fascinating clues to his psychological states and to the genesis of his thought. But although these topics have an interest all their own they are of far less importance than what he actually thought.[1] His most recent biographer makes the extravagant claim that "His philosophy cannot meaningfully be separated from his friendships and quarrels, his illnesses and depressions, his teaching and his letter-writing."[2] It would be odd indeed if one of the foremost masters of German prose were unable to make himself understood save to those who had observed him from the cradle onwards. Walter Kaufmann is quite correct, I think, when he observes that "Nietzsche was a very unusual person, but the most exceptional feature of his life is that he wrote the books that he did in the eighteen eighties."[3]

In the main, the externals of Nietzsche's biography are as prosaic as his inner life was singular. After a rigorous training at the prestigious Schulpforta he began theological studies at the University of Bonn only to abandon them a year later. From Bonn he went to the University of Leipzig where he did masterful work in philology under the eminent Professor Ritschl and began what was to prove a stormy friendship with Richard Wagner. Ritschl was so impressed with his young student that he helped him to obtain a professorship at the University of Basel, a surprising honor for one so young and who had not yet been awarded his doctorate. Ten years later (1879), the thirty-three year old Nietzsche was forced by ill health to resign his post at Basel. He spent the next decade writing in lonely wanderings, searching for a climate that would be suitable to his delicate physiology. On January 3, 1889, he collapsed on a street in Turin and his already wavering mind collapsed within him. The rest was silence. He never recovered his lucidity, and he spent the remainder of his life in the care of his mother and then his sister. Neither had the least inkling of what his philosophy was about although his sister, Frau Elisabeth Förster-Nietzsche, passed herself off as its interpreter and indeed made a considerable amount of money from the sale of his books. Their rise to popularity had coincided almost exactly with their author's decline. He died on August 25, 1900.

Even as a student at Leipzig Nietzsche had begun to grow discontented with philology and to shift his attention to philosophical topics. In his earliest works, *The Birth of Tragedy* and the *Untimely Meditations*, he showed himself to be an acute and canny *Kulturkritiker*. In his next works, *Human, All-Too Human* and *The Dawn*, his interests began to focus on morality and he commenced his critiques of *décadence* and *ressentiment*. These themes were of abiding and ever-increasing interest to him throughout the rest of his philosophical career. He meant to level existing morality, the morality of the herd, of declining life, and to raise on its vacant eminence the will to the Overman.[4] His anti-Christian polemic belongs to the first part of that enterprise. On his view, Christianity cannot but inhibit the enhancement of the type man inasmuch as it enshrines as ideal all that is weak, sickly and declining. Its wretched ideals must be cleared away so that a higher man may be consciously and systematically willed and cultivated. No longer shall he be a mere lucky hit of nature. Nietzsche, a voice crying in the wilderness, would make straight the way of the Overman.

Like the young Hegel,[5] Nietzsche drew a sharp distinction between Jesus (the Jesus of the Gospels) and the creed propagated in his name. "The very word 'Christianity' is a misunderstanding — in reality there has been only one Christian, and he died on the Cross. The 'Evangel' *died* on the Cross. What was called 'Evangel' from this moment onwards was already the opposite of what *he* had lived: '*bad* tidings', a *dysangel*" (A 39). Let us therefore divide our account of Nietzsche's views on Christianity in accordance with this dichotomy.

Nietzsche's views on Jesus are insightful and thought-provoking albeit theologically heterodox and historically dubious. Certainly the former observation would not daunt him a whit. Nor, perhaps, would the latter. "What *I* am concerned with is the psychological type of the redeemer. For it *could* be contained in the Gospels in spite of the Gospels, however much mutilated and overloaded with foreign traits: as that of Francis of Assisi is contained in the legends about him in spite of the legends. *Not* the truth about what he did, what he said, how he really died. . . ." (A 29) With this in mind, let us consider what Nietzsche has to say about Jesus's role, character and teaching.

Just what was Jesus? A prophet: A teacher? A sage? A social worker? Nietzsche insists on viewing Jesus within the context of the Jewish society of his time, and within that context he sees him as a rebel, a kind of "political criminal."

> I fail to see against what the revolt was directed whose originator Jesus is understood or *misunderstood* to be if it was not a revolt against the Jewish Church. . . . It was a revolt against 'the good and the just', against 'the saints of Isreal', against the social hierarchy − not against a corruption of these but against caste, privilege, the order, the social form; it was disbelief in 'higher men', a No uttered towards everything that was priest and theologian. . . . This holy anarchist who roused up the lowly . . . was a political criminal, insofar as political criminals were possible in an *absurdly unpolitical* society. This is what brought him to the Cross. . . . (A 27)

And what manner of man was this "holy anarchist"? Nietzsche's answer is startling. "To make a *hero* out of Jesus! . . . To speak with the precision of the physiologist a quite different word would rather be in place here: the word idiot" (A 29). Here Nietzsche seems to be indulging in a crude and manifestly false calumny: no matter what one thinks of his teachings, Jesus was certainly not an idiot in the physiological sense. To understand what he means here once must bear in mind that, in his later works, he often uses "physiological" where one would expect "psychological." A materialist, Nietzsche was somewhat uncomfortable with the "psyche" in "psychological" and wished to make it perfectly plain that mental phenomena were the results of physical states.[6] One must also bear in mind that his use of the word "idiot" here is tinged with Dostoyevskyan hues. A few pages later he says: "It is regrettable that no Dostoyevsky lived in the neighbourhood of this most interesting *décadent*; I mean someone who could feel the thrilling fascination of such a combination of the sublime, the sick and the childish" (A 31). A man who is "sublime, sick and childish" bears a much greater resemblance to Dostoyevsky's Prince Myshkin than to the sub-imbecile. Still, it is no great compliment to be labelled an idiot even in the Dostoyevskyan sense.

And what of the teaching of Jesus? If the pious among our *lectores benevolentes* have not been taken aback at seeing Jesus described as a political criminal and an idiot, perhaps they will be when they learn that Nietzsche considered his teaching to be, *au fond*, Buddhist.

According to Nietzsche, Jesus's true teaching and legacy consisted not in a set of doctrines but in a *practice*.

This 'ringer of glad tidings' died as he lived, as he *taught* — *not* to 'redeem mankind' but to demonstrate how one ought to live. What he bequeathed to mankind is his *practice*; his bearing before the judges,

71

before the guards, before accusers and every kind of calumny and mockery — his bearing on the *Cross*. He does not resist, he does not defend his rights, he takes no steps to avert the worst that can happen to him. . . . His words to the thief on the cross contain the whole Evangel. 'That was verily a *divine* man, a child of God,' says the thief. 'If thou feelest this' — answers the redeemer — '*thou art in Paradise,* thou art a child of God.' (A 35)

This practice of resignation and acceptance in the face of even the worst that can happen is productive of peace and tranquillity in the here and now, not in some Beyond. It is for this reason, I think, that Nietzsche associates Jesus with Buddhism (A 31, J 202). It is an association rather to the credit of Jesus since Nietzsche, although he is critical of Buddhism, places it far above Christianity. Buddhism, like Christianity, is a religion of decadence owing to its life-stifling doctrines of acquiescence and resignation. But at least it grapples with a real problem, suffering, and not with an imaginary one like sin (A 20). Moreover Christianity, as we shall see, is an expression of rancor and *ressentiment* whereas Buddhism is grounded in "sweetness" and "mildness and gratitude" (WM 154).

In sum, we may say of Nietzsche that although he was critical of Jesus (though much less so than of Christianity), he nonetheless accorded him a certain respect. Jesus's practice of resignation, of submission in the face of suffering is far too passive, far too lacking in vitality for the philosopher of the Will to Power. But at least Jesus's preaching was properly centred; it was a way of living *this* life in *this* world. Unlike his disciples, Jesus did not slander and falsify reality by fabricating fables of a world beyond this one, beyond death (WM 166). Also, Nietzsche believed in the basic nobility of Jesus's character. His Zarathustra, framing a compliment which might appal the pious more than any malediction or

72

anathema, says of Jesus: "He died too early; he himself would have recanted his teaching had he lived to my age! He was noble enough to recant!" (Z I 21)

This may suffice as a brief account of what Nietzsche thought about Jesus. What he felt about him is also of interest although I wish to do no more than call attention to the fact here. Here are some specimen cogitanda for those who, like Nietzsche, "never read a word without seeing an attitude" (A 44). In a letter to the Danish professor Georg Brandes (Nov. 20, 1888), Nietzsche wrote: "I have now told my own story with a cynicism that will make history. The book is called *Ecce Homo* and is a ruthless attack on the crucified Christ. . . ." But less than two months later, in marginally coherent letters to Brandes, August Strindberg and his friend Peter Gast, he signed *himself* "the Crucified."[7] First he told his life story in terms of an attack on the Crucified and then suddenly he was the Crucified. What is the meaning of this bizarre *volte-face*?

Were long repressed religious sentiments from his childhood surfacing in his incipient madness? (His playmates used to call him *"der kleine Pastor."*) Did the fact that the Crucified was called the Son of God appeal to Nietzsche? (In the first days of his lucidity's eclipse he wrote that he, Nietzsche, was to be the successor of the dead God.[8]) Or did Nietzsche feel crucified by the torments of madness? (*"Cruciatus"* is a word which would come naturally to a philologist in pain.) To see clearly into such murk would require a psychological acuity comparable to Nietzsche's own. It is a pity that no Nietzsche lived in the neighborhood of this most interesting *anti-décadent*.

According to Nietzsche, "God is dead" and the Beyond is but a fiction contrived by mendacious calumniators of this world, the one we all live in, the only real world. "To talk about 'another' world than this is quite pointless, provided that an instinct for slandering, disparaging and accusing life is not strong within us; in the latter case we *revenge* ourselves on life by means of the phantasmagoria of 'another', a better life. . . ." (G IV 6)

This being the case, along what paths should a moralist proceed in his inquiries? Obviously the first step is "to separate theological from moral prejudice" and to look for the origin of good and evil *in* the world, not behind it. Thus, Nietzsche poses as his problem: ". . . under what conditions did man devise these value judgments good and evil? *and what value do they themselves possess?*" (GM—V 3)

His fullest answer to the first query is to be found in *On the Genealogy of Morals,* of all his works perhaps the most psychologically acute, wherein he examines what he takes to be the fundaments of *ressentiment* (and, *a fortiori*, Christian) morality. The second receives its most sustained treatment in his vitriolic *The Antichrist.*

To get to the bottom of morality, to unmask the long-shrouded motives of its framers, he proposes to investigate the conceptual origins of the term "good."

> The signpost to the *right* road was for me the question: what was the real etymological significance of the designations for "good" coined in the various languages. I found they all led back to the *same conceptual*

transformation — that everywhere "noble," "aristocratic" in the social sense is the basic concept from which "good" in the sense of . . . "with a privileged soul" necessarily developed: a development which always runs parallel with that other in which "common," "plebian," and "low" are finally transformed into the concept "bad" . . . as yet with no inculpatory implication and simply in contradistinction to the nobility. (GM I 4)

Thus on Nietzsche's view "the good" were originally "the noble," "the masters," "the powerful," "the possessors." "The bad" of course were "the base," "the commons," "the poor." Now it is obvious that these values fell into desuetude quite some time ago. How then did they come to be revalued? And by whom?

Nietzsche's answer is that "the bad," acting out of *ressentiment* at being unable to repay in deed the insults and injuries of their masters, "the good," took the only revenge available to them — a spiritual one. They reversed the table of values by denominating their erstwhile betters "evil," not a mere term of contradistinction but an imputation of unholiness laden with "moralic acid." Themselves of course they called "the good." They accomplished this by lying impotence and weakness into something meritorious, e.g., inability for revenge they called unwillingness for revenge. Listen a moment while Nietzsche's Mr. Rash and Curious relates mutterings from their subterranean workshop where ideals are manufactured. "Now I can hear what they have been saying all along: 'We good men — *we are the just*' — what they desire they call, not retaliation, but 'the triumph of *justice*'; what they hate is not their enemy, no! they hate 'injustice,' they hate 'godlessness'. . . ." (GM I 14)

But are they telling the truth? Not at all, says Nietzsche. In reality they are vengefully awaiting a chance to bring home their curses to their masters, the mighty whose spittle they have to lick (not from fear, mind you, but because their God has bid them obey the authorities). "These weak people — some day or other *they* too intend to be the strong, there is no doubt of that. . . ." Indeed, precisely what constitutes the bliss of the Christian paradise is its gratification of *eternal hate*. Nietzsche finds this hate laid bare in some stern and even savage words of Thomas Aquinas and Tertullian, words seldom bruited about in our ecumenical era of universal love.

We might guess at the bliss of the Christian paradise, says Nietzsche, but it is better to have it explicitly described for us by Aquinas. "'The blessed in the kingdom of heaven,' he says, meek as a lamb, 'will see the punishment of the damned *in order that their bliss might be made more delightful for them.*'"9

Tertullian is far less restrained, gloating wildly over the inevitable fate of the Christians' foes. Imagining himself gazing down into the Pit from the heights of heaven, he sternly exclaims:

> *Which sight gives me joy? which rouses me to exultation?* — as I see so many illustrious *monarchs* whose reception into the heavens was publicly announced, groaning now in the lowest darkness with great Jove himself . . . governors of provinces, too, who persecuted the Christian name, in fires more fierce than those with which in the days of their pride they raged against the followers of Christ.10

And so on and so on. The "moral" of the *De Spectaculis* whence this is taken is that Christians should refrain from attending the cruel games in the public arenas, especially since the Faith will one day provide them with the unsurpassed spectacle described above.

So much then for love of one's enemies, for not hating them but the ill that they do. What lies behind the weak and ignoble's revaluation of the old "master morality" is nothing but *ressentiment* and the desire for vengeance against the strong, against "monarchs" and "governors of provinces."11

But "slave morality," the morality of *ressentiment*, is not merely a subterranean form of revenge: it is also a means of defense against the strong and masterful. These latter, not much schooled in deceit and cunning since they seldom needed them, have rather ingenuously taken the calumnies of the weak and lowly to heart. Thus they have developed a "bad conscience" about the strengths which are native to them as manifestations of ascending life, of life which has turned out well. Having been gulled into thinking that their strengths are reprehensible, they can no longer exercise them with their former lordly *hauteur*. They can only give them rein at the price of lacerating their consciences.[12]

In a parable: lambs have decreed that if wolves are hungry, they must not eat lambs. It would be evil and unholy to do so. Curiously enough, the wolves take this to heart and for want of other sustenance take to gnawing at *themselves*. As Arthur Danto points out, this is a phenomenon of *moral optics*. The masters, by accepting the value table of the slaves, have been persuaded to evaluate themselves *from the slaves' perspective*.[13] As a result, they endeavor to stifle their strengths, to emasculate themselves, in short to invert the alchemists' dream and transmute gold into base metal.

Now there is an obvious objection to Nietzsche's account thus far. It is contained in the reply of Socrates to the following contentions of Callicles:

> In my opinion those who framed the laws are the weaker folk, the majority. And accordingly they frame the laws to their advantage, and so too with their approval and censure, and to prevent the stronger who are able to overreach them by saying that to overreach others is shameful and evil. . . . But in my view nature herself makes it plain that it is

right for the better to have an advantage over the worse, the more able over the less.[14]

Socrates aptly retorted that the majority seems to be more able and powerful by nature since by its laws it has been able to restrain the "stronger." One might well make the same point against Nietzsche. Since, as a matter of fact, the supposedly weak exponents of *ressentiment* or slave morality have utterly triumphed over the master morality of strong, noble types, have they not shown themselves to be stronger than their adversaries and thus the true masters?

I think that Nietzsche's answer to this objection can be inferred from the following passage wherein "Rome" symbolizes the older, nobler ideal and "Judea" the morality of *ressentiment*. "Which of them has won *for the present*, Rome or Judea? But there can be no doubt: consider to whom one bows down in Rome itself today. . . ." (GM I 16) In other words, the struggle is not over.[15] Of a certainty it is not over since there are thinkers such as Nietzsche who are willing to challenge the values of impotence on behalf of those of strength.

This struggle is not merely for the hearts and minds of men, important though that may be. Nor is it merely to create a favorable climate for the arising of a higher type of man, important though that is. It is over the value to be assigned to the world, to reality itself. The following passage makes this plain and indeed neatly summarizes much of the discussion so far.

[In the] sphere of moral values one cannot find a greater contrast than that between a *master morality* and the morality of *Christian* value concepts: the latter developed on a soil that was morbid through and through (The Gospels present us with precisely the same physiological types that Dostoyevsky's novels describe), master morality ("Roman," "pagan," "classical," "Renaissance") is, conversely, the sign language of what has turned out well, of *ascending* life, of the will to power as the principle of life. Master morality *affirms* as instinctively as Christian morality *negates* ("God," "beyond," "self-denial" — all of them negations). The former gives to things out of its own abundance — it transfigures, it beautifies the world *and makes it more rational* — the latter impoverishes, pales and makes uglier the value of things, it *negates* the world. "World" is a Christian term of abuse. (W—Ep)

These claims bring into prominence the second of Nietzsche's questions noted earlier, the question of the value of the valuations uncovered. Precisely what is the worth of this slave rebellion in morals? His answer is evident from the tenor of his remarks cited so far: Christianity is an unutterable and almost unmitigated calamity. Not only does it calumniate the world and thwart the finest flowering of the type man, it actively sides with the weak and ill-constituted.

One should not embellish or dress up Christianity: it has *waged a war to the death* against this higher type of man, it has excommunicated all the fundamental instincts of this type. . . . Christianity has taken the side of everything weak, base, ill constituted, it has made an ideal out of *opposition* to the preservative instincts of strong life; it has depraved the reason even of the intellectually strongest natures by teaching men to feel the supreme values of intellectuality as sinful, as misleading, as *temptations*. The most deplorable example: the depraving of Pascal, who believed that his reason had been depraved by original sin, while it had only been depraved by his Christianity! (A 5)

Nietzsche's objection that Christianity actively succours the weak and ill-constituted sounds strange to most modern ears. The ancients would almost certainly have concurred that such a religion was objectionable. This is apparent when one considers that Aristotle held a doctrine of "natural slavery" and that deformed infants, if they were not exposed, grew up to be objects of universal derision and even loathing. However, we moderns, whose moral beliefs are for the most part imbued with a certain humanitarianism, may find this objection of Nietzsche's less than telling. After all, are not the weak and ill-constituted the most in need of assistance?

Nietzsche's retort would almost certainly be that although they may be the most in need of succour, they are the least deserving of it. To fully grasp this point one must appreciate his criticisms of pity, an affect which he anathematizes at every opportunity.

> Pity on the whole thwarts the law of evolution, which is the law of *selection*. It preserves what is ripe for destruction; it defends life's disinherited and condemned; through the abundance of the ill-constituted of all kinds which it retains in life it gives life itself a gloomy and questionable aspect. (A 7)

But may it not be said in defense of the weak and ill-constituted that, at least, they are right to fear the hard *virtù* of the higher, nobler man? And if the basis of their fears is sound, why should they not take steps to defend themselves? Why should they rein in their cunning, their *ressentiment*, their mendacious tongues? In short, why should not *their* strengths be allowed to express themselves as strengths?

First of all, it is not clear that Nietzsche's intention is to entreat the lowly to cease plying their wiles. In fact it would seem extremely odd if the prophet of the higher man were to petition the "impotent" to make way. If, as is claimed, the higher man is stronger, why does he not simply make his way through them?

Nietzsche's criticisms of the weak and lowly are best read not as entreaties, and still less as attempts to reform them[16] ("The last thing I should promise would be to improve mankind" [EH–V]), but as a declaration of war. Let the foe come on!

Secondly, although the lowly are right to fear, they are not thereby justified.

> One may be quite justified in continuing to fear the blond beast [lion?] at the core of all noble races and in being on one's guard against it: but who would not a hundred times sooner fear where one can also admire than *not* fear but be permanently condemned to the repellent sight of the ill-constituted, dwarfed, atrophied and poisoned? (GM I 11)

This Olympian contempt of Nietzsche's, far from being a surd or *brutum factum* and hence inexplicable, can be said to rest on prior aesthetic and physiological judgements. On his view, the fact of the matter is that the "dwarfed, atrophied and poisoned" are *ugly*. Indeed it is as "The Ugliest Man" that present day man, herd animal man, the assassin of God is represented in *Thus Spoke Zarathustra* (IV 7). Is it not an objection to a creed that it makes men repellent? And are we not right to be repelled by the repellent? Moreover, Nietzsche sees in their *décadence* a sickness (WM 39–45). It is a morbidity, a degeneration of the instincts and the organism, a "falling away" from health, from the integrity of one's nature. A creed which poisons and sickens men is a contagion. Who would dare defend it as such? And surely the physician needs no excuse for seeking *to reduce the number* of the sick.[17]

In sum, Nietzsche repudiates Christian values in terms that are as unambiguous as they are unrestrained. "I call Christianity the *one* great curse, the *one* great intrinsic depravity, the *one* great instinct for revenge for which no expedient is sufficiently poisonous, secret, subterranean, *petty* — I call it the *one* immortal blemish of mankind. . . ." (A 62) Sprung from the sickly soil of *ressentiment*, the Gospel of the lowly makes low.

Nietzsche on Paul and Luther

In addition to a general critique of Christianity as a manifestation of *décadence in extremis* Nietzsche has some interesting remarks regarding the changes it has undergone through the centuries, especially those wrought by Paul and Luther. A quick glance at these will serve to round out our exposition of his views.

He never refers to Paul save in terms that one reserves for one's *bête noire*. In particular, Paul grossly falsified and perverted the legacy of Jesus by conjuring up the *ignis fatuus* of an after-life.

> In Paul was embodied the antithetical type to the 'bringer of glad tidings,' the genius of hatred. . . . *What* did this dysangelist not sacrifice to his hatred! The redeemer above all: he nailed him to *his* Cross. The life, the example, the teaching, the death and the meaning and the right of the entire Gospel — nothing was left once this hate-obsessed false-coiner had grasped what he alone could make use of. . . . The invention of Paul, his means for establishing a priestly tyranny, for forming herds [was] the belief in immortality. . . . (A 39)

The malicious lie of immortality has a variety of baneful effects. It robs the actual world of its value by making one look beyond it.

One considers oneself a mere sojourner or wayfarer in this, the only real world, while deludedly anticipating a future life. It relegates actions in the here and now to the status of mere means, and to an illusory end at that ("salvation"). Worse yet, it was the avenue by which Paul was able to introduce *ressentiment*, hatred and plebian crassness into the teaching of Jesus. We have already seen, in Aquinas and Tertullian, the congenial role of immortality in the revenge fantasies of the impotent. On Nietzsche's view it is no less agreeable to the essential *baseness* of the Christian. He has invented for his own long-home a place far different from his enemy's dungeon of torment; ignoble through and through, he wants to be *well paid* for his love. Nothing less than an *eternal reward* will compensate him for foregoing the pleasures of poisoning his neighbor and violating his wife.

Knowing as we do that Luther had a profound respect for the writings of Paul, we should not be surprised to find that he too falls within the compass of Nietzsche's maledictions.

This is not to say that Nietzsche was ill-disposed to Luther as a person. In fact he even expresses "*My kind of 'pity'*" for Luther; a man of "precious capabilities," he squandered his immense forces on problems that were none (WM 367). Nor does he hold that "calamity of a monk" personally responsible for his fatal world-historical role: by attacking Catholicism Luther *restored* it (and Christianity with it) at the very moment when, under popes of the Borgias' ilk, it was waning and perishing. "The Catholics would have good reasons to celebrate Luther festivals, to write Luther plays" (EH III 3; cf. FW 358, 148–9).

Harder to overlook, though, are Luther's misology and his uninspired exaltation of faith over works.

Nietzsche has a low estimate of faith in general inasmuch as he feels that "convictions are prisons," that is, "The believer is not free to have a conscience at all on the question of 'true' and 'false'. . . ." (A 54) As for faith as opposed to works, "One must practice deeds, not the strengthening of one's value-feelings; one must first have some *ability* — the Christian dilettantism of Luther. Faith is a *pons asinorum*" (WM 192; cf. M 22). The last sentence provides us with the clue as to *why* faith was exalted over works: Luther and his kind were profoundly convinced of their utter incapacity for Christian *works*. Thus they built themselves this "bridge for asses" so that salvation might depend on what was in fact within their power.[18] "Faith over works" is a confession of weakness.

Furthermore, placing a premium on faith often results in the disparagement of reason on the grounds that it is naturally inferior to faith and in fact destructive of it. Luther's writings positively teem with evidences that misology was no small part of *his* faith. The following, cited by Kaufmann in his book on Nietzsche (pp. 350—351), may suffice as examples:

> Whoever wants to be a Christan should tear the eyes out of his reason. . . .

> Reason and the wisdom of our flesh condemn the wisdom of the word of God.

> Here [in matters of faith] you must part with reason and not know anything of it and even kill it; else one will not get into the kingdom of heaven.

The lack of *delicatezza* and *nuance* in such forthright misology is not at all out of place in the "ingenuous and bearlike subalterns' faith" of "northern barbarians" like Luther (J 46). But for Nietzsche such an abasement of reason is quite unacceptable. It stems from a will to self-deception: he who "tears the eyes out of his reason" either wants *not* to see what he does in fact see, or else to see what he does not. At the bottom of faith is the inability to bear the world as it is and the desire to lie one's way out of it.

Thus, for Nietzsche, Paul and Luther's falsifications of the legacy of Jesus are dark chapters indeed in an *Historia Calamitatum* whose gloom keeps thickening towards the end. Through them life's center of gravity has been shifted from the real world to an imaginary one, action has been denigrated, faith born of the inability to act exalted, and its concomitant, misology, belched forth among the nations.

This concludes our exposition of Nietzsche's critique of Christianity. The soundness of his critique is quite another matter. It has apparent weaknesses. For example, atheism seems to be taken for granted, and is it not a crude genetic fallacy to suppose that by exposing the motives of Christianity's originators one refutes their claims? Surely why something is said is a separate issue from the truth of that something.

The discussion of these matters will be deferred to Chapter Four. I shall say here, though, that the consideration of Nietzsche's atheism leads, through his views on value and truth, to the heart of the difference between him and Pascal, and that in general there is more strength in Nietzsche's attack on Christianity than there appears to be.

CHAPTER THREE

FRIEDRICH AND BLAISE

This chapter treats the Nietzsche/Pascal relationship from two perspectives: from that of an encounter between men and that of a clash between ideas. Consequently, it poses two sets of distinct though not unrelated questions. Those which perforce occupy the background in a study of this sort concern the elective affinities which exist between the two thinkers despite their antipodal views, and the reasons for which it was *Pascal* whom Nietzsche so often chose to speak and spar with. The second set of queries concerns the particulars of Nietzsche's responses to points of Pascal's brief for Christianity and the justice of those responses.

Some may object that to ask qustions of the latter sort is to show oneself to be hopelessly naive in dealing with texts and, moreover, to stack the deck against Nietzsche. For although Pascal wrote as an apologist and theological controversialist, this was not how Nietzsche read him. On this view, Nietzsche, a fine connoisseur of the human spirit, reacted to the psychology of Pascal and to the acuity of his insights as a moralist and *not* to Pascal the theologian. Thus, to rate Nietzsche as though he were responding to Pascal's apologetics would be grossly unfair. It would be to score him for a game which he refused to play, for did he not consider argumentation for and against the truth of Christianity to be in principle futile?

> The problem of truth [regarding Christianity] can slip away to hiding places of all kinds; and the greatest believers may finally avail them-

selves of the logic of the greatest unbelievers to create for themselves
a right to affirm certain things as irrefutable — namely, as *beyond* the
means of all refutation — (this artifice is today called "Kantian Criticism"). WM 251; cf. 252 and W—Ep.

This objection will not do, however. Despite avowals that Christianity cannot be proven or disproven, Nietzsche does in fact
develop a case against the truth of Christian theism; its details
were stated in the previous chapter. His arguments are of course
not of the metaphysical variety which might be eluded by the
"artifice" of Kantian Criticism. Rather, they are historical and
moral. And as we shall see in this chapter, at times he does indeed
engage Pascal the apologist head on, though never for long. It is
indisputable, therefore, that Nietzsche makes an intellectual as
well as an aesthetic case against Christianity — he would have it
to be false as well as deformed and deforming — and so one may
well ask if he succeeded. My own view, whose particulars will
emerge in due course, is that Nietzsche's quick ripostes to specific
Pascalian points are generally anemic, but that his over-all case
against Christianity is more robust than believers are wont to
realize or would like.

The Anti-Christ on the Subject of his Jansenist Friend

We do not know precisely how carefully or at what length Nietzsche read Pascal. There are good grounds for thinking that Nietz-

sche's French was not very good,[1] so it is unlikely that he had read him extensively in the original. He did have a translation entitled *Gedanken und Briefe* which followed the edition of Faugère (1844). Faugère, it will be remembered, based his edition largely on *pensée* no. six in which Pascal's argument is divided into a first part showing "The wretchedness of man without God" and a second showing "The happiness of man with God." It is safe to say that Nietzsche did not have a *scholarly* knowledge of Pascal, although this is not to say that he did not understand Pascal and his *idées maîtresses* very well indeed. Still, we should bear in mind that Nietzsche's declaration "I do not read but *love* Pascal" (EH II, 3) could very well mean that he loves Pascal *instead of* reading him.

When considering Nietzsche's views on Pascal some attention must be paid to chronology. As J.R. Dionne points out,[2] he seems first to have focused his attention on Pascal's apologetics, then on his skepticism and finally on his asceticism. This is true, but only in general and for the most part.

Early on he seems to have been impressed with Pascal principally as an insightful analyst of the human condition. For example, in the *Untimely Meditation* on David Strauss (1873) he adopts Pascal's account of distraction.[3] But in *Human, All-Too Human* (1878) and *The Dawn* (1881) his by now frequent references to Pascal are largely concerned with his apologetics and with his own rather summary counters.

Some of his disagreements with Pascalian doctrine are, though not unimportant, nonetheless far from crucial to Pascal's over-all case for Christian theism. Pascal lists "The holiness, sublimity and humility of a Christian soul" as one of Christianity's "proofs" (no. 482) — a classification which would strain the credulity of many a believer to say nothing of a *libertin's*. He also avers that he believes only histories whose witnesses are ready to be put to death, and that he considers the survival and growth of the Christian religion in the face of continuous attack to be a clear manifestation of divine power (nos. 882 and 281). Nietzsche, without naming Pascal, notes all three ideas in *The Dawn* (73) and, not surprisingly, finds them less than conclusive.

A much more serious disagreement occurs over the morality of the hiddenness of God. Pascal defends this divine attribute at some length (e.g., in nos. 149 and 446), but Nietzsche considers that such a God would be grossly unjust.

> *God's honesty*. A god who is all-knowing and all-powerful and who does not even make sure that his creatures understand his intentions — could that be a god of goodness? Who allows countless doubts and dubieties to persist, for thousands of years, as though the salvation of mankind were unaffected by them, and who on the other hand holds out the prospect of frightful consequences if any mistake is made as to the nature of the truth? Would he not be a cruel god . . . ? . . . All religions . . . take astonishingly *lightly* the duty to tell the truth: they as yet know nothing of the duty of God to be truthful towards mankind and clear in the manner of his communications. On the 'hidden god,' and on the reasons for keeping himself thus hidden and never emerging more than halfway into the light of speech, no one has been more eloquent than Pascal — a sign that he was never able to calm his mind on this matter. . . . He sensed a piece of immorality in the '*deus absconditus*' and thus was very fearful and ashamed of admitting it to himself: and thus, like one who is afraid, he talked as loudly as he could. (M 91)

Here it seems that Pascal has supplied Nietzsche not only with a target to attack but with the petard to hoist it. For Pascal too speaks of the duty of God to man, though perhaps he was reacting against Descartes' *malin génie* rather than having second thoughts about the hidden God. In any event, "God owes it to men not to lead them into error" (no. 840; cf. no. 841). Perhaps Pascal would say that God has been even more clear in his dealings with men than he is obliged to be, for considering man's radical depravity (a consequence of the Fall), God's obligations to men are slight; hence, whatever he might do for us is largely supererogatory. Nonetheless, Nietzsche's argument is apt to be very persuasive to anyone whose view of the God/man relationship is less lopsided. And its logical force is considerable, concluding as it does that the Christian God is credited with incompatible attributes, benevolence and hiddenness, and hence is a *contradicatio in adjecto*. Note too that it is an attempt at a moral refutation of the Christian God — that is, an attempt to debunk him of the very kind used by early Christian writers against the gods of classical antiquity. In short, to all appearances Nietzsche is belaboring the Christian God with a fistful of rods obligingly cut and pruned by Pascal and other Christian apologists. (The strength of arguments which, like M 91, maintain that the concept of a given deity is internally inconsistent is discussed in the Appendix to this volume.)

In a note written around 1885 Nietzsche attacks Pascal's most celebrated argument, the wager, as an argument from *fear*, a common though historically inaccurate interpretation (cf. n. 45 to Chapter One). Nor is the wager apt to persuade any longer.

> Even granted that the Christian faith might not be disprovable, Pascal thinks, nonetheless, that in view of a *fearful* possibility that it is true, it is in the highest degree prudent to be a Christian. Today one finds, as a sign of how much Christianity has declined in fearfulness, that other attempt to justify it by saying that even if it were an error, one might yet have during one's life the great advantage and enjoyment

of this error: — it therefore seems that this faith ought to be maintained for its tranquillizing effect. . . . This hedonistic turn, the proof from *pleasure*, is a symptom of decline: it replaces the proof from *strength*, from that which overpowers us in the Christian idea, from *fear*. (WM 240)

Nietzsche never specifically assesses the wager's merits as an argument though he derides it on two counts. As we see in the passage above he takes it to be founded on *fear*, a motive superior to the vulgar craving for pleasure but still quite unacceptable. "Being moral means being highly accessible to fear," he wrote in 1881, adding that the weakness of this fear was "really contemptible" (X, 374). Secondly, he dismisses the whole topic of the salvation of the soul as uninteresting. This is not surprising, of course, given that the *salus* Nietzsche enjoins on men is health, soundness, and not salvation. But the reasons he gives in the following passage are surprising. "We are no Pascals, we are not especially interested in the 'salvation of the soul,' in our own happiness, in our own virtue. — We have neither the time nor the curiosity to rotate about ourselves in that way" (WM 426). Perhaps this is in part a rejection of eudaimonism — Nietzsche is striving, not for happiness, but for greatness of soul. Yet, in the face of his emphatic disinterest in one's *own* salvation, happiness and virtue, one is tempted to utter a *tu quoque* and remind Nietzsche that neither he nor the type of man he prefers is remarkably "altrocentric." Indeed, the astonishing depth of self-knowledge which his works betray suggests that he "rotated about himself" well nigh continually. But be that as it may, on his view undue egocentrism and susceptibility to fear would seem to be the reefs on which the wager founders.

92

Like the great majority of Pascal's modern readers, Nietzsche gives scant attention to the Biblical "proofs,"[4] the very heart of Pascal's largely historical and empirical case for the Christian religion. However, he does have one argument whose effect would be to repudiate the Pascalian claim of perpetuity. The "attempt to pull away the Old Testament from under the feet of the Jews — with the claim that it contains nothing but Christian doctrines and *belonged* to the Christians as the *true* people of Israel" is an "unheard of philological farce" (M 84). Even if the Jews were not standing or trampling on the Old Testament, as his quaint figure seems to suggest, the fact remains that if Nietzsche were correct here then there would be no continuous tradition of belief in the Messiah stretching from the first men to the last — only jarring sects, one of whom has robbed the other.

Nietzsche would doubtless label the prophecies, whether used to support the claim of Jesus's divinity or the continuity between the testaments, philological farces as well. "Wherever a piece of wood, a rod, a ladder, a twig, a tree, a willow or a staff is mentioned, it is supposed to be a prophetic allusion to the wood of the Cross. . . . Has anybody who asserted this ever *believed* it?" (M 84) On miracles, the chief of Pascal's other "proofs," he is silent.

We may conclude our survey of Nietzsche's reactions to Pascal the apologist with a look at what he called *"der Hauptfehler Pascals."*

Pascal's capital mistake: He supposes that he proves Christianity to be true because it is necessary. This presupposes that a good and truthful providence exists which ordains that everything necessary shall be true. But there can be necessary errors! (XI, 72)

Perhaps Nietzsche has the wager in mind here. Even if it is necessary to profess belief in God and to act accordingly to have a chance for the greatest happiness, one's belief may not be true. This is fair enough as argument but inexact as exegesis. For as we saw above,[5] there are very good reasons for thinking that the *Christian* God is not the subject of the wager. Nor is the wager to prove that belief in a god is true, but only that it is eminently prudent to hold it as true. And even if these points did not hold, it would be a mistake to reduce Pascal's case for Christian theism to the wager. If, then, *"der Hauptfehler Pascals"* refers to the wager, one could well argue that the mistake is not Pascal's.

Another possibility, and a very likely one in my view, is that Nietzsche was unduly influenced (not to say misled) by the form in which the *Pensées* were encountered by him, that is, in Faugère's arrangement. It considers the great divisions of the argument to be man's misery without God and his happiness with him. This of course makes it look as though Pascal is enjoining the *libertin* to embrace Christianity as something necessary to his happiness. But as we saw in Chapter One, Pascal's apologetic strategy is by no means reducible to this. On this interpretation too, a close reading of Pascal would show that *"der Hauptfehler Pascals"* is not Pascal's. A more exact knowledge of Pascal would have spared Nietzsche the slight ignominy of this Quixotic joust at an imaginary foe.

So much, at least for the present, for Nietzsche's reactions to Pascal the apologist. What of his immediate though short-lived successor, Pascal the skeptic?

I do not think that Nietzsche ever considered Pascal to be first and foremost a skeptic, but at the time of *Beyond Good and Evil* (1886) he was giving a fair amount of thought to skepticism and Pascal often came to mind as a ready example. "[T]he faith of

Pascal . . . resembles in a gruesome manner a continual suicide of reason — a tough, long-lived wormlike reason that cannot be killed at a single stroke" (46). Apart from the bad faith (self-deception) of faith, the chief problem with a Pascalian "*sacrifizio dell'intelletto*" would seem to be its essential *morbidity*.

> [T]he skeptic, being a delicate creature, is frightened all too easily; his conscience is trained to quiver at every No, indeed even at a Yes that is decisive and hard, and to feel as if it had been bitten. . . . For skepticism is the most spiritual expression of a certain complex physiological condition that in ordinary language is called nervous exhaustion and sickliness. (J 208)

Needless to say, no such skeptic could ever fulfill the Nietzschean ideal enshrined in the doctrines of *amor fati* and the Eternal Recurrence.[6] One cannot say a triumphant Yes! to life, even to the point of being willing to live it again, its best *and* foulest moments, if one is the timid, sickly, exhausted being described by Nietzsche.

But is Pascal in fact a skeptic, let alone one of the sort Nietzsche describes in J 208? Here again, Nietzsche's appreciation of Pascal is a bit inexact. For although there is a large vein of skepticism running through the *Pensées*, as we saw in Chapter One it would be a mistake to say that Pascal was himself a skeptic. For on his view nature confounds the skeptics just as they confound the dogmatists (# 131). Even the notorious *cela vous abêtira* towards the end of the wager is less misologic than it first appears. This is the "proof" by "*la machine*" according to which one stupefies oneself, or, just as literally, becomes like an animal (apparently of the Cartesian kind); that is, one has recourse to habit to smooth one's difficulties in acquiescing to belief — but this is to take place only *after* one has given intellectual assent to it.

In his latest works Nietzsche usually considers Pascal as an extreme ascetic, a self-lacerator and self-tormentor, a great sayer of No! to life.

> One should never forgive Christianity for having destroyed such men as Pascal. . . . What is it we combat in Christianity? That it wants to break the strong . . . that it knows how to poison and sicken the noble instincts until their strength, their will to power turns backward, and against itself — until the strong perish through orgies of self-contempt and self-abuse: that gruesome way of perishing of which Pascal provides the most famous example. (WM 252; cf. 932 and EH II, 3)

That Pascal was very much an ascetic is clear from his sister's biography even if allowance is made for a bit of hagiographical hyperbole. "It was not possible for him not to use his senses at all. But when he was obliged by necessity to afford them some pleasure, he had a marvelous talent for turning his mind away so that it took no part in it" (p. 22). He saw impurity in the caresses bestowed on his sister by her children, an opinion he prevailed upon her to share, although with some difficulty (p. 28). As for self-contempt, it is clear that he meant his famous "*le moi est haïssable*" (no. 597; cf. no. 618) even though he had written as eloquently of man's *grandeur* as of his *bassesse*. I do not of course mean to imply that there is nothing in the ego and in the senses which one would do well to oppose. But Pascal puts one in mind a bit of Plotinus, of whom Porphyry says in the first words of his *Life* that he seemed ashamed to be in the body at all. Even the asceticism of some of the Desert Fathers had its lighter side. For example one Sarapion, vaunting his hardihood at body-mortification to his fellows, is said to have taunted them with "I'm deader than you are."[7] Asceticism of this sort smacks of an athletic contest; Pascal's, at least as represented by his sister and a few of his *pensées*, is grim, dour, implacable. Nietzsche's dismay is not difficult to fathom.

This may suffice as a sketch of the main lines of Nietzsche's overt reactions to Pascal and Pascalism. But precisely what is the nature of his relationship to Pascal the man, and what underlies and conditions it?

We should not be surprised that, despite their widely differing views, Nietzsche is far from feeling any rancour or animus towards Pascal. Nietzsche declared himself well disposed even towards his enemies: as a man "beyond good and evil" he might hate (oppose) his enemies, but not despise them. Indeed, "You must be proud of your enemy. . . ." (Z I 10) But Pascal, whom Nietzsche professed to *love* (EH II 3), is no enemy but a friend and blood-brother. In a passage of some beauty, Nietzsche includes Pascal in the little circle of thinkers with whom he holds most and highest converse. The presence of Plato and Rousseau and Montaigne affords additional evidence that Nietzsche was attracted to minds that he reacted against. For Nietzsche, unlike for many among his opposition, orthodoxy was not a requirement for communion.

> *The journey to Hades.* — I, too, have been in the underworld, like Odysseus, and shall be there often yet; and not only rams have I sacrificed to be able to speak with a few of the dead, but I have not spared my own blood. Four pairs it was that did not deny themselves to my sacrifice: Epicurus and Montaigne, Goethe and Spinoza, Plato and Rousseau, Pascal and Schopenhauer. With these I must come to terms when I have long wandered alone; they may call me right and wrong; to them will I listen when in the process they call each other right and wrong. Whatsoever I say, resolve, or think up for myself and others — on these eight I fix my eyes and see their eyes fixed on me. (MA II 408)

What, however, is the *ground* of the patent esteem in which Nietzsche held Pascal? And of the affection?

Raisons d'un Effet

If anything, Nietzsche's feeling for Pascal is over-determined: it is a phenomenon behind which we find a number of sufficient-seeming reasons.

Perhaps the chief is that which is implicit in WM 252: the feeling of an art lover before a defaced masterpiece,[8] the tragic spectacle of the ruin of something great. Perhaps, as tragedies are wont to do, this one aroused a certain pity in the beholder. One recalls that pity for the higher man was Zarathustra's ultimate temptation (Z IV, 2 & 20). It may well be that Zarathustra resisted it better than his creator.

Another reason is voiced by Nietzsche himself in a letter to Georg Brandes:

> I prize his [Dostoyevsky's] work, on the other hand, as the most valuable psychological material known to me — I am grateful to him in a remarkable way, however much he goes against my deepest instincts. Roughly as in my relation to Pascal, whom I almost love because he has taught me such an infinite amount — the only *logical* Christian.[9]

What are his intellectual debts to "the only *logical* Christian"? Some would be debts that the great majority of intelligent readers would incur, e.g., an awareness of the power and ubiquity of distraction and of the empire imagination exercises. Others would be peculiar to Nietzsche and a few kindred spirits, e.g., a full revelation of the extent to which Christianity is noxious based on the harm done to this most instructive victim.

Still other grounds of indebtedness to Pascal are rather more conjectural. W.D. Williams thinks that he might well be beholden to him for the germ of his conception of "master" and "slave" moralities.[10] Pascal never tired of pointing out that human justice was founded on *force*: men, unable to fortify justice, have simply justified force (cf. esp. nos. 81 and 82). This may have helped Nietzsche to his insight that power (or want thereof) is the ultimate basis of moral valuation. And on the stylistic plane, Nietzsche's penchant for the aphorism might be traceable to Pascal. Nietzsche certainly thought highly of the aphoristic form in general ("A good aphorism is too hard for the tooth of time" [MA II 268]), and of Pascal's use of it in particular ("The profoundest and least exhausted books will probably always have something of the aphoristic and unexpected character of Pascal's *Pensées*" [WM 424]). But if Pascal was influential on these points, he may have been a partial influence at most. Just as Nietzsche's reading of Theognis or Thucydides would have sufficed to acquaint him with the notion that force is what underlies moral assessments, so his reading of La Bruyère, La Rochefoucauld, Goethe, Lichtenberg and others could well have enamored him of the aphorism.

But there is more behind Nietzsche's feeling for Pascal than gratitude of the sort one feels for the best of one's teachers. There is also, despite their profound disagreements, an affinity of souls, a call of like to like between the two. In part this affinity may be the result of ideas which they happen to share, but beyond this there is a kinship in outlook, temperament and sensitivity.

Both are masterful stylists, an obvious but important point. They were both remarkable for their facility with the aphorism, a difficult form requiring an unusual capacity to distill thought as well as the more vulgar talents of the sloganeer and ad man. It is a form well suited to convey the paradoxical, to sting the reader out of his dogmatic torpor, and both used it thus with telling effect. Both wrote a prose which is supple, clear and pointed, curt or drawn out as the occasion demands, but which is neither a mere tool for the conveyance of cognitive content nor the "pure folly" of "good style *in itself*" (EH III 4).

Pascal's carefully wrought *Provincial Letters* are a landmark of French prose. They expound an abstruse subject, grace, with astonishing clarity and biting wit. In an age in which almost all men and women of any intelligence took a lively interest in theological controversy, it won immediate recognition. As for the *Pensées*, I find them even more enchanting *because of* their unfinished form. Jean Guitton is right, I think, when he says: "How tempting it is for us, who cannot imagine the Apology finished, to prefer it just as it is! Its unfinished character confers upon it the beauty of omission, the *eternal silence* of lacunae, variety, and still more the possibility of being reborn in each consciousness, even those the most removed from Pascal's."[11]

German philosophy has long had a reputation for being bombastic, turgid and teeming with solecisms, a labyrinth in which Ariadne's thread, if it is there at all, is entwined with long strings of pronouns of opaque reference and overtopped by a clutter of verbosity. This reputation, as readers of Kant and Heidegger may suspect and as readers of Hegel and the impenetrable Krause know for sure, is not entirely undeserved. But Nietzsche's reputation is deservedly quite different. As he prophesied (EH II 4), he is considered one of the foremost masters of the German language. The summits of his prose as well as of his thought are to be found in the often oracular, sometimes intoxicated, quasi-biblical *Thus Spoke Zarathustra*.

On his own view he started out badly. The "Attempt at Self-Criticism" which he appended to his first book, *The Birth of Tragedy* (1872), fourteen years after its first appearance, speaks disparagingly of it as "an impossible book . . . badly written, ponderous, embarassing, image-mad, image-confused" (3).[12] But he soon learned to write concise, pointed, delightful prose, prose with *presto*, the quality he admired so much in Petronius (J 28).

Both Nietzsche and Pascal hold that man is in effect "corrupt" and must be "redeemed." In Pascal of course this is just standard Christian doctrine, albeit with a strong Augustinian tinge. In Nietzsche, on the other hand, man has been corrupted by the emasculating, poisonous morality of *ressentiment*. He has fallen away from life and health and hence is *décadent*. Redemption consists in recovering health in its fullness. This is not possible in very many cases — only a few can come to exemplify humanity at its highest, soundest, most vital and triumphant. And it is by them that mankind can be "redeemed" in the sense that *its* existence would be justified by *theirs*. The production of these higher men would be humanity's redeeming feature, the means of its deliverance from contempt. One's task therefore is to will the Overman and to cultivate conditions favorable to his arising.

Both were great intuitive psychologists, a point of resemblance which need scarcely be belabored. Nietzsche is the uncoverer of *décadence* and *ressentiment*, and his appeciation of human types, for example the ascetic (cf. esp. GM III), is canny indeed. It is largely on account of his psychological acuity that he is such a

101

fine *Kulturkritiker. Homer's Contest* (1872), in which he assesses the significance of the pervasive spirit of competition (*agon*) in the life of classical Greece, provides a fine example of his talents in this line. As for Pascal, he is second to none in his ability to see through human pretention, a truth amply illustrated by his analyses of distraction, indifference, justice, imagination, et al. And it is on account of their psychological finesse that their rhetoric, their *art de persuader*, is so sure and subtle. They knew their audiences intimately, that is to say they knew men, for rhetoric demands this more than virtuosity in the juggling of the classical rules and figures (with which they were both familiar).

Both are prototypes of what we would today call existentialists. They are concerned with man primarily as an individual, and they have a keen sense of the human condition as a predicament in which men are faced with momentous choices.

According to Pascal, man finds himself alone in a dumb universe stretching from the infinitely small to the infinitely great. Not knowing whence he came nor whither he goes, he must nonetheless *act* as though he did. Consequently, he must choose (or "wager") whether or not his life's past, present and prospect are to be understood as things whose ultimate significance derives from within or without the world, from man himself or from God. There is no neutral ground; one must choose.

Nietzsche's account of the human predicament has it that post-classical man has stupefied himself in order to dull the hard edges of his existence. Unable to bear the arbitrariness, the meaninglessness of reality, he has mendaciously invented "another," a "better" world, a "spiritual" realm in which dwelleth provident Deity. To those who prostrate themselves before this monumental lie existence seems less harsh. No longer must one bear the meaninglessness of suffering as well as the suffering itself. Now one

102

"knows" that suffering is only a test, a trial of one's faith. In other words, the wind has been tempered to the newly-shorn lamb. Men, by myth-making, have reduced the terrors and disquiets evoked by the world to a level commensurate with their courage.

Now the situation of at least some modern men is this: they begin to stir from the long half-dream; they begin to rend the Judaeo-Christian veil of lie; they realize that "God is dead." The choice confronting them is whether or not to cease opiating themselves, to cease sweetening reality, to *dare* to know even though the truth be hard and severe. Also, it is incumbent on them to choose the kind of man to be willed henceforth — the herd animal for whom life, unfalsified, is too much to bear, or something *beyond* him: strong, vital, courageous in the face of terrible truths. This is very much in the existentialist spirit: choose the type of man you would be, will it and then become it. Or, in the Pindaric formula so dear to Nietzsche, "Become what you are."

I have reserved for last what may be the most important of the grounds for Nietzsche's affinity with Pascal.

The first and more important is pure and simple aesthetic awe. It would be hard to believe that Nietzsche, who was nothing if not a connoisseur of men and an aesthete in a very large sense of the term, was not moved by the sublime interior drama of a soul at once so like and unlike his own.

The second concerns Pascal's courage. "Dare to know," an injunction from Horace, has long been a cherished commonplace. In the German Enlightenment it served the Society of the Friends of Truth as a motto, and Kant saw it as the motto of Enlightenment itself.[13] It is an imperative that Nietzsche cherished too, and that could fittingly have served as his device. For it is a commonplace with him that what is needful for attaining truth, especially though not exclusively in morals, is courage. "How

103

much truth does a spirit *endure*," he asks in his last work. "How much does it *dare*? More and more that became for me the real measure of value" (EH–V 3). I dare say that one of the things he admired and loved in Pascal was that he, too, was not afraid to face some very hard "truths." Pascal looks straight at hell and eternity, abysses and infinities, and though he is shaken he still stands and looks. He does not turn away, and he does not falsify the world into something sweeter, softer, easier to bear. If anything, Christianity of Pascal's sort may make the world *harder* to bear with its doctrines of predestination and freely (arbitrarily?) bestowed grace for a few elect. It is small wonder that Nietzsche drew a sharp distinction between Pascal's fearful faith and the faith of later days (WM 240). But it would be a great wonder if Pascal's courage in the face of what seemed to him very hard truths indeed did not strike a responsive chord in Nietzsche.

Transition

Pascal's blood runs in my veins, said Nietzsche (XXI, 98). But how different a turn it took in him! Pascal, desperately sincere and with heart racing, agonizes over the question of Christianity's truth. For him it is *the* question since one's eternity, one's all may depend on the answer. But Nietzsche, despite his preoccupation with Pascal, gives this question scant attention. He attacks Christianity at length and in detail, but most of his criticisms are

104

directed against its *value*. The question of its truth receives much less attention, and that desultory in the extreme. This emphasis reflects an attitude which Pascal found not only alien but incomprehensible (cf. esp. no. 427; also nos. 150 and 163). In short, Nietzsche's oft-proclaimed respect for Pascal never induced him to grant the case for Christianity's historical and metaphysical truth a very serious hearing.

It would be easy to explain this phenomenon from a psychological and biographical point of view. Nietzsche's anti-metaphysical bias made it impossible for him to view Christianity as a "live option" for belief, and the fact that he was trained as a philologist rather than as a philosopher doubtless affected the kinds of questions he tended to ask himself. "Is this claim true?" seems to have occured to him less frequently and forcefully than "What attitudes does this claim betoken? Is the soil whence it sprang healthy or infected?" and so forth.

But to explain Nietzsche's impatience with Christianity's pretentions to truth is one thing, to justify it another. What logical considerations in Nietzsche's philosophy might there be which would warrant it? If his critique of Christianity is to be more than an aesthetic indictment of the man it tends to produce, a charge which will be examined in the next chapter, this question must be answered.

There are two possible answers in Nietzsche. The first is that the question of a conception's value is of more importance than that of its truth. This startling claim will be dealt with in the next chapter in the context of a discussion of Nietzsche's atheism.

The second would be that Nietzsche's own critique of Christianity's pretentions to truth, although cursory, suffices as a compelling or probable counter-proof. For when one has refuted a view one is of course not obliged to examine its defences in detail: they *must* be inadequate, else what they defend could never have been overthrown. To attack them now would be a senseless redundancy; there is no need to undermine what has already been toppled.

But is this the case? Does Nietzsche have a strong case against the *truth* of Christian theism? This is an important question, for from a rhetorical point of view his anti-Christian polemics will be less than devastating if, from the outset, he assumes the opposition to be bereft of evidence; and from a logical point of view he will simply "beg the question."

It certainly does not *appear* that Nietzsche has given a sound critique of Christianity, for as I noted at the end of the last chapter, his case against it seems open to some obvious and crushing objections. In particular:

1) He tries to overthrow Christian morality, and hence the whole edifice of Christian belief (since enjoining adherence to disvalues so rank is incompatible with divinity [A 47]), by exposing the unworthy motives of its supposedly impotent and *ressentiment*-driven founders. But this is an out-and-out genetic fallacy.

2) Atheism is an axiom with Nietzsche, not a theorem. Hence he "begs the question" against Christianity.

As we shall see in the following chapter, these objections are powerful but not unanswerable. Yet even when the answers are made, I do not think that his case against Christianity is really sufficient, and so the question of its truth remains open. And when we probe the foundations of Nietzsche's atheism and come to his stance on the value of truth we shall see, I think, that he was further removed from Pascal (and from philosophy itself) than he seems to have realized, and maybe further removed than he should have been.

106

CHAPTER FOUR

THE NIETZSCHEAN CASE EXAMINED

Nietzsche's Natural History of Morals: A Genetic Fallacy?

It is a commonplace in logic that showing how or why a certain belief is or might come to be held does not ordinarily[1] show it to be true or false. To argue as though it did is to commit a genetic fallacy, for by ignoring the difference between the truth value of belief and the genesis of belief one ignores the fact that beliefs stand as true or fall as false on their own merits.

Nietzsche himself was decidely piqued when certain of his critics traced his ideas back to their supposed origins and considered them thereby dealt with and disposed of.[2] But does he not proceed in the same way against Christianity? After all, his account in GM I of how and why Christian valuations came to be serves as an attempt to refute them and the doctrines embodying them. For he concludes that Christian value-claims are false, asserting as they do that disvalues are values, and from this would follow the falsity of Christian belief as a whole if one supplied the obvious premise that the acute disvalue of ideals would give the lie to any allegations of their divine origin or sanction.

Fallacious or sound, this line of argument — the *exposé* of the genesis of a belief — deserves our close attention. It is a very prominent one in anti-Christian polemics — Hume, Freud, Marx and Feuerbach all used it — and Nietzsche set great store by it.

> *Historical refutation as the definitive refutation.* — In former times, one sought to prove that there is no God — today one indicates how the belief that there is a God could[!] *arise* and how this belief acquired its weight and importance: a counter-proof that there is no God thereby becomes superfluous. (M 95)

Is such reasoning cogent? One's first impulse is to concur with J.P. Stern's assessment that "Nietzsche's arguments . . . are always at their weakest where he offers 'ways of becoming' not merely as explanations but as the ground of value judgements."[3] Or of truth judgments, one might add. But is this obvious appraisal correct?

Before attempting an answer, it would be well to make clear whether his argumentation is to be understood as counting against the *truth* or *value* of Christian ideals and belief. He himself is more concerned with their value, but let us consider what force his natural history of morals would have against their truth as well.

I   Proof of Untruth?

If Nietzsche's natural history of morals is taken as intended to show the falsity of Christian ideals and doctrines, then it certainly does commit the crude genetic fallacy described above. The motives on account of which Christianity came to be held entail nothing with regard to the *truth* of its historical, metaphysical or value claims. I may believe in a wicked Abominable Snowman who eats little boys only because my Abominable Governess liked to frighten me with such stories when I was a child. But whether or not such a being exists is unconnected with the genesis of my belief that he does.

Still, if my only reason for thinking that this Yeti pedophage exists as advertised is the authority of my governess and my trust in her, and if at some time she is proved to me to be a veritable sink of improbity and falsehood, then my belief has no adequate foundation even though its *falsity* has not been shown. In a like manner, Nietzsche's natural history of morals may be understood as showing, not the falsity, but the unjustified character of Christian belief — a weaker but still very damaging objection.

One need only consider the Christian faith as resting not so much on a chain of evidence as on a chain of trust in the veracity of one's forebears.[4] If we believe on the word of our trusted fathers, and they on the word of theirs and so on, we find that the ultimate repositories of our trust are the primitive Christians. We may choose to understand Nietzsche as trying to break the fiduciary chain at its first link by showing that the first Christians were utterly unworthy of being taken at their word.

Nietzsche would argue that the primitive believers had no reasons, only motives (and very ignoble ones) for believing and speaking as they did. But is this right? After all, to show that the first Christians had motives is not the same as showing that they lacked reasons. Even if they were venting their spleen against the upper orders and hoping to protect themselves from the ravages of the masterful, their beliefs may have had a reasonable basis. Perhaps they had seen wonders worked, or prophecies fulfilled, or, say, had heard God on the road to Damascus.

Nevertheless, a Nietzschean might well respond that a) the burden of proof is on him who would show that they *did* have solid reasons for their belief — if they expect later generations to incorporate Christianity into their systems of belief, the onus is on them as innovators — and b) *this burden of proof is unbearable* once the motives of the earliest Christians have been unmasked. For what are traditionally adduced as the reasons for their belief (miracles, prophecies, some contact with God) are things for whose truth we have no evidence but their word, and which in themselves seem highly improbable. But owing to their vested interest in propagating a certain type of value-system, and owing to their known baseness, their word must be viewed as eminently suspect. In short, if they are the lying rabble described by Nietzsche, their word is a most inadequate foundation for the belief of later generations.

We may note in passing that Pascal would surely have appreciated the force of this line of reasoning; it is, after all, one he used on behalf of Christianity. He was quite conscious of the importance of witnesses (*"témoins"*) to the case for Christianity (cf. nos. 204, 436), and held that, had all the Jews been converted, there would have been only *"témoins suspects"* (i.e., partisan witnesses) to the truths about Christ.[5] Nietzsche's argumentation, understood as I have suggested, meets Pascal on his own ground, namely that of the historical and the moral rather than the metaphysical.

In sum, Nietzsche's natural history of morals is, if considered as directed against the warrant of Christian belief, far from falling into the irrelevance of the genetic fallacy and far from consisting of mere *ad hominem* invective against the framers of Christian ideals. Rather, it is a serious and pointed attempt to show that being a Christian means being possessed of astonishing epistemological naiveté.

110

Nonetheless, his argumentation suffers from a crippling defect: it relies on historical claims which are, to all appearances, simply false.[6]

Far too little attention has been paid by commentators to the empirical truth of Nietzsche's natural history of morals despite the following facts: a) His account is put forward by him as an empirical claim, for he bases it on etymological evidence which is supposed to point to conceptual transformations which actually occurred; b) His account, understood as an attack on the trustworthiness of the framers of Christian ideals, relies on the historical truth of his *exposé* of their character and motivating forces; and c) His account is contradicted on important points by what we know of the period he must be taken to be describing.

First of all, Nietzsche depicts Christian ideals as springing up in a noble, heroic society whose own values they subsequently subverted. Nothing could be further from the truth. Christianity did not arise (or spread) in a society of Homeric heroes. Tiberius, Caligula and Nero are hardly Agamemnon, Menelaus and Diomedes. The well-born of the early Empire yearned to traverse the *cursus honorum* for lucre rather than for glory. And by the time Christianity was beginning its rise to prominence in the early third century, the Roman Empire had become a vast, stifling bureaucracy, increasingly lacking in vitality of all kinds. The bane of the lowly in those days was the avaricious army of civil servants and the ubiquitous Imperial spies (*agentes in rebus*); these are hardly the lordly, masterful, eminently autonomous men whose spittle the lower orders have to lick in GM I.

Nor did Christianity propagate values so very different from those of its host culture.

Nietzsche says that Christianity shifted the focus of importance from the here and now to a metaphysical realm and afterlife. But very many pagans in the early Christian era severely disparaged the material world — consider Marcus Aurelius and the Stoics, and Plotinus and his followers to name only a few famous examples. Moreover, many pagans already believed deeply in some kind of immortality. The soul's survival of the body's corruption was a commonplace to the Platonists, both "neo" and "paleo," and a staple of widespread mystery cults such as those of Isis and Mithra.

Thirdly, Christianity does not seem to have grown, as Nietzsche claimed, in a soil of lower-class hatred for the mighty of the earth. Its early growth was indeed greatest among the lower orders, but this does not mean that it was a plebian revolt against privilege. Rather, its initial lack of appeal to the generally well-educated upper classes seems to have had an intellectual ground, a ground very similar to the one we have been crediting to Nietzsche. As E.R. Dodds points out:

> To anyone brought up on classical Greek philosophy, *pistis* meant the lowest grade of cognition: it was the state of mind of the uneducated, who believe things on hearsay without being able to give reasons for their belief. St. Paul, on the other hand, had represented *pistis* as the very foundation of Christian life. And what astonished all the early pagan observers, Lucian and Galen, Celsus and Marcus Aurelius, was the Christians' total reliance on unproved assertion. . . .[7]

As evidence of plebian hatred of the upper classes, Nietzsche cites the final paragraphs of the *De Spectaculus* of Tertullian, an author not notable for his restraint, and selectively quotes

Aquinas in a way which distorts his view so as to make it appear malignant (see n. 9 to Chapter Two).

Far more typical than Tertullian's attitude toward those in power is Justin Martyr's in his *First Apology*. Addressed to the emperor Antoninus Pius, it is calm, respectful and judicious. Pius is enjoined to weigh the case against persecuting the Christians and the case for their creed against any accusations and to decide as seems right and fair to him. There is a faint whiff of Tertullian when Julian mentions that if Pius persists in injustice towards the Christians, God's wrath awaits him (68). But this mention is so casual as to bespeak indifference rather than *ressentiment*. Indeed, it is not clear whether Justin hopes to sway Pius by a quick argument *ad baculum* or whether he only means to do his duty by warning a rash traveller of a danger down the road. Like the great majority of his co-religionists, Justin, far from evincing rancor towards the authorities, was prepared to follow the Biblical injunction to render Caesar his due.

So much for Nietzsche's natural history of morals construed as an attack on the truth of Christian belief or as an attack on the fiduciary chain which, one suspects, is the actual basis of the belief of most Christians at most times. It fails, being either irrelevant or wanting in truth or trustworthiness itself at crucial points. But how does it fare when used as Nietzsche primarily intended it?

II Proof of Disvalue?

At this point the genetic fallacy is, strictly speaking, no longer possible; there can be no confusion between truth and genesis if what is at issue is not the truth of belief but its value. But we can still assess the cogency of Nietzsche's case for the disvalue of Christian ideals.

Before undertaking this a fairly lengthy preliminary is in order, however.

There is a problem which any appraisal of Nietzsche's critique of Christianity as a disvalue must face, namely, the fact that he seems simply to presuppose the value of his own ideal of man. Precisely why is the noble, strong-and-self-willed *briseur d'obstacles* a good man, a man turned out well, and a better man than less robust souls? Why, like Alexander, should one take Achilles as a model?

I can think of three defenses of the value of the Nietzschean ideal. I do not know that any of them is entirely adequate; the last might be.

The first defense would simply be that Nietzsche's value-criterion needs no defense. On this view, when Nietzsche says "What is good? All that heightens the feeling of power, the will to power, power itself in man. What is bad? All that proceeds from weakness" (A 2), he is not catechizing us, he does not expect us to repeat *his* responses. No! This is *his* good and bad; it is up to us to find ours — if we have the stuff for it.

> But he has discovered himself who says: This is *my* good and evil: he has silenced thereby the mole and the dwarf who says: 'Good for all, evil for all.'

114

. . . .
  'This — is now *my* way: where is yours?' Thus I answered those
who asked me 'the way'. For *the* way does not exist!
  Thus Spoke Zarathustra.   (Z III 11; cf. J 260, 21)

But despite this conception of the higher type of man as a value-
creator, Nietzsche often spoke as though values were in some sense
objective and the same for all. For example, he calls Christianity
"the *one* great curse, the *one* great intrinsic depravity" (A 62). To
call something an *intrinsic* depravity does not sound like value-
legislating, like *assigning* a value to something. It implies rather the
recognition of (dis)value. In short, "intrinsic depravity" is a function of that in which it inheres, and not of some external be-
stower of value. But in any event, if we consider Nietzsche's ideal
for man to be merely his own pet value-creation, then obviously
his criticisms of opposing ideals are trivialized. Exponents of rival
ideals need only say, "That is *your* way; this is *mine*." This is not a
very satisfactory position for Nietzsche, who is nothing if not a
polemicist, to be in.

 The second defense is cogently put by John Wilcox:

> If he [Nietzsche] is right, we all seek power, first and most funda-
> mentally; and we all *must* — this is the nature of a living being. But if
> that is true, then, in a sense, the norm of power does not have to be
> justified; we are confronted with a fait accompli — in ourselves. It is as
> if we had all accepted the norm and cannot now reject it. It *is* our
> standard and it *must* be — there is no alternative to it. Those like Nietz-
> sche, who talk openly about it, acknowledge that their aim is power;
> Christians and "no-sayers" of all stripes deny that their aim is power,
> but it *is* anyway and it will continue to be. If Nietzsche's theory of the
> will to power as a factual, psychological or biological hypothesis is
> true, then his norm of power, as a standard of value, does not need
> justification; there is no alternative to it.[8]

This is ingenious, but I think that it fails as a defense for three reasons.

First, as Wilcox points out, it presupposes the empirical truth of Nietzsche's claim that living things *are* the will to power. But this is an empirical hypothesis which has never been proven. Thus, this line of defense merely substitutes one *ipse dixit* for another.

Secondly, if we all use power as a norm regardless of what we say on the subject, then Christians and "no-sayers" can only be taxed with hypocrisy for claiming to do otherwise. But this makes nonsense of Nietzsche's polemics: he charges them, not with tartuffery, but — as in Pascal's case — with espousing and living by and propagating life-stultifying ideals. In short: if men cannot but act according to the norm of power, why does Nietzsche exhort them to do so and castigate them for not doing so?

Thirdly, this defense grounds the concept of good (or value) in a human nature which is fixed: we are and must be the will to power, hence what furthers this will is good (at least from a teleological perspective). But of course what is natural is not necessarily good. For example, one's critics may be by nature obtuse but it is hard to see how they are improved thereby. Nor is it obvious that our nature is made of adamant. Thinkers as diverse as Pico della Mirandola and Sartre have seen man, not only as having a certain plasticity in his nature, but as being capable of creating his nature himself. As long as this is an open question, and it is at present, why should we be content to live at the level of our nature as described by Nietzsche if there might be a chance of rising above it? In fine, both the characterization of man as will to power and the fixity of his nature are moot at the least.

The third defense, and the one I think Nietzsche would prefer, is aesthetic. He seems to have thought that moral valuations are, *au fond*, aesthetic ones. For example, he characterizes his valua-

116

tion of life as "purely artistic" (GT—V 4), and the problem with *ressentiment* morality is that it thwarts the development of fair specimens while it "condemns one to the repellent sight of the ill-constituted, dwarfed, atrophied and poisoned" (GM I 11; cf. A 7). Or, to put the point more broadly, "Only as aesthetic phenomena are existence and the universe forever justified" (GT 5).

I do not think that this defense would trivialize his position by rendering it purely subjective and idiosyncratic because I think it patent that many of our aesthetic judgments are objective and factual. In essence, my position is the one Hume put forward in "Of the Standard of Taste." There he correctly observed that he who held Ogilby to be as great a poet as Milton would maintain an extravagance, just as if he were to maintain that a mole-hill were as high as Teneriffe.[9] The same would be true of him who asserted that a thoughtlessly crushed styrofoam coffee-cup was as fine a piece of sculpture as the *Pietà*. These may fairly be adduced as paradigm cases of objective aesthetic judgment. For practical reasons, objectivity may be difficult or even impossible of attainment in comparative judgments between objects of nearly equal merit. But the fact that paradigm cases of objectivity exist shows that aesthetic judgments are not entirely about their utterer.

In other words, Nietzsche might well defend the values embodied in his ideal as follows: "Compare Pascal with me. He actually loved sickness; I prize health. He disapproved of the pursuit of excellence;[10] I enjoin it on myself and others. He hated his '*moi*'; just read *Ecce Homo* for me on *moi*! In fine, Pascal said 'No!' to the world whereas I say, not only 'Yes!' but 'Encore!' He who holds that Pascal is a better turned-out man than I maintains an extravagance, pure and simple. I suppose he rates the scribblers in his newspaper higher than Racine!" In short, perhaps Nietzsche simply has good taste in men. This is scarcely an air-tight defense of his valuations, but it is very far from no defense at all.

And as far as I can see, there is more than a little to be said on behalf of Nietzsche's ideal of man. Some caricature it; some pooh-pooh it; some recoil from it in righteous indignation. Nonetheless, we should not be blind to what is fine in it. I think that Lord Macaulay appraised the masterful man perfectly when he wrote:

> The character [of the masterful man], thus formed, has two aspects. Seen on one side, it must be regarded by every well constituted mind with disapprobation. Seen on the other, it irresistibly extorts applause. The Spartan, smiting and spurning the wretched Helot, moves our disgust. But the same Spartan, calmly dressing his hair, and uttering his concise jests, on what he well knows to be his last day, in the pass of Thermopylae, is not to be contemplated without admiration. To a superficial observer it may seem strange that so much evil and so much good should be found together. But in truth the good and the evil, which at first sight appear almost incompatible, are closely connected, and have a common origin. It was because the Spartan had been taught to revere himself as one of a race of sovereigns, and to look down on all that was not Spartan as of an inferior species, that he had no fellow feeling for the miserable serfs who crouched before him, and that the thought of submitting to a foreign master, or of turning his back before an enemy, never, even in the last extremity, crossed his mind.[11]

Nietzsche too recognizes this duality in the masterful man, and he is willing to suffer it. One may be quite justified in fearing the blond beast at the core of all noble races, but who would not a hundred times sooner fear where he can also admire than be condemned to the repellent sight of the ill-constituted? (GM I 11)

At this point we will bring our excursus to an end and return to the question we deferred at the beginning of this section, namely, what success does Nietzsche's natural history of morals have when construed as an argument for Christianity's disvalue?

Since at least some grounds can be adduced for his ideal for man we might concede it for the sake of argument. We might make the even larger concession of allowing him to take it as an unprovable axiom, a position he suggests in W—Ep. But even with such an allowance his arguments fall short, it seems to me.

For them to be successful one would have to concede, not only the superiority of his ideal for man, but the empirical truth of his natural history of morals. If Nietzsche were right in his claim that Christian values and doctrines were framed by vermin of the vilest instincts to safeguard and to aggrandize their ilk, and if he were right in insisting that such men should be suppressed and their antipodes willed and cultivated, then we would have very strong inductive grounds for thinking that Christianity was indeed a disvalue. Under such conditions it would fail to be a disvalue only if Christians were inept, unable to match means to the ends they will. But even if one grants the superiority of the Nietzschean ideal, there is, as we have seen, scant reason to grant the empirical truth of his natural history of morals.

Someone might object that Nietzsche's natural history need not be empirically true to function. Why not construe it as an expository device, much like the "state of nature" in Locke, Hobbes and Rousseau? Why not understand it as saying that Chrisitan values are *as if* they were the expression of anti-aristocratic animus, just as we sometimes speak of civil society *as if* it resulted from a contract made by men in the state of nature? But obviously this would degrade the natural history of morals from an argument purporting to establish disvalue to an illustration of supposed disvalue, and this would ignore the empirical basis alleged for it in GM.

Another problem with Nietzsche's case for Christian disvalue stems from what might be called "natural result." Even if the worth of his ideal is granted, is it the case that Christianity really serves to thwart its attainment?

Pascal would seem to be a case in point for Nietzsche, but was he really, as Nietzsche thought, a potential higher man ruined by Christianity? One might well argue that a man made of the stuff *Übermenschen* might be wrought of would have a greater resistance to anti-life influences. Perhaps Christianity, by figuring in a "natural selection" process of sorts, ensures the vigor and purity of those few who do attain higher-manhood.

Moreover, does Christianity necessarily enfeeble the will to power in a man? What of Cromwell, Innocent III, Richelieu, Charles d'Anjou and innumerable other Christian churchmen, soldiers and statesmen? I dare say that their faith was genuine; certainly it was not mere pretence. Yet their will to power does not seem to have been notably subdued. Of course they are not typical Christians, but then the masterful man will always be an exception.

Does Christianity make its devotees anti-world? Some have been, although Christian epicures are not unheard of either. On a more serious level, although Christianity includes the world and the flesh as prime sources of temptation, love of the world has traditionally been found to be compatible with it. St. Francis of Assisi comes to mind as a ready example, he of the lyrical *Cantico del Sole* and *Laudes Creaturum*, he who tenderly calls sun and wind brother and moon and water sister. Many contemporary Christians are so far from being anti-world that they see poverty and hunger as far greater evils than sin, one expects. And does not

Jehovah, in "Genesis," declare that the world is not only good but very good ("*Panta lian kala*")? How true is it, then, that Christianity naturally tends to produce a type of man abhorred by Nietzsche — the world-slanderer?

Does Christianity inhibit the development of aristocratic spirit and greatness of soul? If it does, it is odd that a great part of the aristocracy of post-classical Europe — a class with a code of honor all its own, first chivalric and then gentlemanly, a class notable for its *hauteur* and *dédain* (not to say *mépris*) *vis à vis* the lower orders — has been staunchly Christian.

And, most important, does Christianity, which is essentially heteronomous ("Thy will be done," not mine), stifle the autonomy which is so prominent in the Nietzschean ideal?

This is the heart of Nietzsche's quarrel with Christianity. On the face of it the conflict is irresolvable, yet it *might* be tractable since, at the level for which the Christian ultimately strives, the autonomy/heteronomy distinction breaks down. Dante illustrates this beautifully in his *Commedia*. Early in the *Inferno* his will is often at odds with God's; for example, if he could, he would succour some of the sinners God has condemned. But as he progresses through Purgatory and Paradise his will converges with God's to join it as a tributary joins its stream, so to speak, at the Beatific Vision in the last canto. Dante and God remain distinct, but not Dante's will and God's will. Autonomy is a Christian as well as a Nietzschean ideal, but the Christian feels that his will must be rehabilitated before autonomy is safe and right.

In sum, it is very much a moot point as to whether Christianity does tend to produce the kind of mewling Uriah Heeps (J.P. Stern's phrase) that Nietzsche says it does. And even a glance at the types of men Christianity has in fact produced entitles one to some very severe doubts regarding the claim that it is essentially and unavoidably opposed to the arising of the masterful. These things, taken in conjunction with the empirical deficiencies of his natural history of morals and any lurking doubts concerning the value of his ideal for man, vitiate his critique of Christianity as a disvalue.

Atheism and Truth: Begging the Question and Lèse Majesté?

One of the things which makes Nietzsche eminently worth reading is his radical willingness to call into question the dogmas of the philosophers as well as those of the many. But does he not have dogmas and *partis pris* of his own? In particular, it has seemed to many commentators that his atheism is fixed and dogmatic, mere assertion.[12] But if this is the case, then of course he has "begged the question" against Christian theism. Is his atheism axiomatic?

As we saw above,[13] Nietzsche's earlier writings contain some arguments or at least argument-sketches against the truth of (Christian) theism. For example, in M 95 he argues that once we understand how the concept "God" *could* arise (*entstehen konnte*) a (metaphysical?) counter-proof is unnecessary. Presumably this odd claim means that if one can "save the phenomenon" of belief in God with a purely natural hypothesis, no recourse need be had to a supernatural one. But to be at all effective, this argument would have to show that the natural explanation is a more probable account of how the concept "God" *did in fact arise*, and for this empirical confirmation is needed. One cannot simply say that the natural explanation, as natural, is *ipso facto* more probable than any supernatural one without begging the question against the latter. The natural alternative must be shown to be more than a mere possibility. It is not enough to cry, as did Statius's Capaneus, *"Primus in orbe timor fecit deos!"* One would have to show that the gods *were* born of men's fears. No one would demand near-apodictic proof for such a thesis; a "smoking gun" (or stylus) would be virtually impossible to find even if the thesis were true. But at the very least a natural history of morals would have to be shown to be more probable than its rivals, and this would require, not only the saving of the phenomena, but substantial support from historical and psychological disciplines. Without it, the theist needs no retort save the famous Laconic reply to a long Athenian string of hypotheticals: "If."

A more powerful charge against Christian theism was also noted above, viz., that a God who is both hidden and good is a contradiction in terms (M 91). But this argument, though strong, is not developed, and it relies on implicit definitions of "hiddenness" and "benevolence" that a theist could choose not to accept. Thus, the Christian, when pressed, can always maintain that the God disproven by the argument is not his God.

In his later works Nietzsche foregoes arguments for atheism, and in his very latest he describes his own disbelief as axiomatic.

> "God," "immortality of the soul," "redemption," "beyond" — without exception, concepts to which I never devoted any attention, or time; not even as a child. Perhaps I have never been childlike enough for them?
>
> I do not by any means know atheism as a result; even less as an event; it is a matter of course with me, from instinct.[14]   (EH II 1)

I think, then, that despite some early arguments or argument-sketches for atheism, Nietzsche does in effect beg the question against Christian theism. For his own disbelief, considered not as a biographical matter but as a tenet of his philosophy, does not seem to rest on these. He always considers Christianity as a mere sociological phenomenon, and hence something to be judged in terms of its effects. Atheism is "a matter of course," as he says in EH; he seems not to have entertained as a real possibility that Christianity might be what it claims to be — God-inspired.

Nor can one argue that, since the burden of proof is on the theist, Nietzsche need only remain unconvinced rather than argue for *his* position. This would work only if one could show that the other side, contrary to its claims, has not in fact discharged that burden of proof. But Nietzsche does not do this in his writings. He did not dismiss the case for Christian theism unheard, but he seems to have rendered a verdict after the defense had little more than cleared its throat. The question is effectively begged.[15] Or, as Nietzsche once said, though I dare say he did not have himself in mind:

> There is a point in every philosophy when the philosopher's "conviction" appears on the stage — or, to use the language of an ancient Mystery:
> > *Adventavit asinus,*
> > *Pulcher et fortissimus.*[16] (J 8)

But why is Nietzsche so little interested in the theism/atheism question, and in the general question of Christianity's truth as opposed to that of its value? The principal reason would seem to lie in his frank and startling admission that he considers a conception's *value* to be *more important than its truth.*

124

Philosophers are not, on the whole, prone to idol worship. And yet, as Nietzsche pointed out,[17] there is one idol (his word for "ideal") before which the bosoms of philosophers are wont to tremble with pious enthusiasm: Truth. It is the sovereign ideal of philosophy, but Nietzsche seems to be guilty of a certain *lèse majesté*. For despite his frequent encomia of truth, and despite the assurances of commentators such as Walter Kaufmann and Karl Jaspers that it was his highest faith and ruling ideal,[18] Nietzsche did not shrink from calling the value of truth into question.[19]

> For all the value that the truth, the truthful, the selfless may deserve, it would still be possible that a higher and more fundamental value for life might have to be ascribed to deception, selfishness and lust. (J 2)

Nor does he shrink from answering this question: what is more important than even truth is *value for life*.

> The falseness of a judgment is for us not necessarily an objection to a judgment; in this respect our new language may sound the strangest. The question is to what extent it is life-promoting, perhaps even species-cultivating. (J 4)

In this passage Nietzsche is referring to the "fictions of logic" and not to moral judgments. He does, however, extend this subordination of truth to value for life to the moral realm. His critique of Christianity is a striking case in point.

He expends a great deal of ink and fury inveighing against Christianity as a crime against life, a disvalue of the first magnitude, but he seldom argues at any length against the truth of Christian belief. Thus, one might infer from his practice that the question of its value is the preëminent one and that of its truth secondary.

But such an inference, though reasonable, is superfluous. He is quite explicit about the matter.

> Hitherto one has always attacked Christianity not merely in a modest way but in the wrong way. As long as one has not felt Christian morality to be a capital crime against life its defenders have had it all their own way.[!] The question of the mere "truth" of Christianity — whether in regard to the existence of its God or the historicity of the legend of its origin, not to speak of Christian astronomy and natural science — is a matter of secondary importance as long as the question of the *value* of Christian morality is not considered. (WM 251)

We see, then, that Nietzsche need not be understood as indulging in hyperbole when he says that "If this God of the Christians were proved to us to exist, we should know even less how to believe in him" and "so absurd a God would have to be abolished even if he existed" (A 47, 52).

This exaltation of a conception's value for life over its truth as a criterion of acceptability for belief is, to put it mildly, breathtaking in its radicalism.[20] Indeed, to the devotees of truth it must sound not only radical, but downright demented. But is it? Or is Nietzsche right? Is truth an ideal of the second rank? Is a conception's value more important?

It is tempting to say that, for Nietzsche, these are really only pseudo-questions occasioned by his practice of speaking with the vulgar now and then. For although he sometimes opposes the value of a conception to its truth, strictly speaking he held that truth itself was only a measure of value.[21] According to him, all of our judgments, including those of logic, are fictions insofar as they are not true in the correspondence sense. They are most emphatically *not* isomorphic with independently existing states of affairs. However, certain fictions have been affirmed as "true" for pragmatic reasons, the most notable of which is that they aid in the preservation of those who affirm them. For example, species-members who generalize on the basis of past experience stand a better chance of surviving than those who do not. Those of our ancestors who, having narrowly escaped the onrush of a sabre tooth tiger, did not promptly decide to avoid other sabre tooths were doubtless not long for this vale of tears. On the other hand, those less latitudinarian souls who quickly stereotyped sabre tooths as being irremediably addicted to dining at their expense stood a much better chance of dying full of days and progeny. The import of this is clear: ways and categories of thinking which have a greater survival value than their contraries will, for that reason, be affirmed as "true" and bequeathed as such to subsequent generations.

In short, one might say that Nietzsche's claim that a conception's value is to be given more weight than its truth means, when understood in the context of his epistemology, that judgments of value must be decisive since truth claims are really only value claims. We have nothing but a conception's value to consider when we are deciding whether or not to incorporate it into our system of beliefs.

However, it does not appear that Nietzsche can be consistently understood in this way. His pragmatic theory of truth is both possessed of serious internal problems and at odds with other elements of his philosophy.

It has often been noted that, although his explicit theory of truth is a pragmatic one, he often speaks in a way which presupposes the correspondence theory of truth.[22] Consider, for example, his celebrated doctrine of the Will to Power. Nietzsche is by no means as precise or as detailed in his characterization of this concept as one would like, but this much is quite clear: the Will to Power is an ontological concept. Although it has not been conclusively proven that all things, both living and unliving, *are* the Will to Power, nonetheless "one has to risk the hypothesis." Indeed, "the conscience of method demands it. Not to assume several kinds of causality until the experiment of making do with a single one has been pushed to its utmost limit. . . ."[23] In other words, Nietzsche, although an avowed anti-metaphysician, sometimes uses language in an attempt to describe the real. He proposes the doctrine of the Will to Power, not as an aid to species-preservation or enhancement, but as an account of the *Grundstoff* of the real.

A greater problem lies in the fact that his pragmatic theory of truth is ultimately unintelligible unless the correspondence theory is presupposed. For example, if we take the true as being that which is of value for life, how are we to explicate the truth about "life"? Shall we say, "That concept of 'life' will be accounted true which is most valuable for life?" Of course not; such a claim would be on a par with the "*virtus dormitiva*" response of Molière's doctors. But this means that Nietzsche's theory of truth is in the quite unenviable position of not being able to settle on the truth about the key term ("life") in its truth-criterion. To apply his truth-criterion some antecedent notion of what life truly is (in the correspondence sense) is wanted. A similar difficulty arises when his pragmatic theory of truth is asked to provide the truth conditions for the propositions which comprise *it*. For example, would Nietzsche hold the proposition "Evaluations occur when truth-claims are made" to be true in the correspondence sense or in his pragmatic sense? If the former, then his theory of truth is incomplete since it does not cover all propositions; if the latter, then his pragmatic theory does not describe what actually occurs when judgments of truth are made. It itself is but a fiction — a very valuable one, perhaps, and hence "true," but a fiction nonetheless. Nietzsche, however, propounds his pragmatic theory as though it *actually described* how truths are made.[24] Indeed, its justification is made to consist in precisely this. But how can Nietzsche's pragmatic theory describe what actually occurs in the truth-forging process unless *it* is true in the correspondence sense?

As a result of these problems with his pragmatic theory of truth, we cannot use it to mitigate the paradoxical nature of his claim that a conception's value is of more importance than its truth. We cannot simply say, "Nietzsche's claim, understood at a deeper level, only means that judgments of value must be decisive since truth-claims themselves are merely value-claims." Such a retort is no longer an option once one realizes that his pragmatic theory of truth is neither consistent with the rest of his philosophy nor free from serious internal difficulties.

But suppose we take Nietzsche to mean that truth in the *correspondence* sense should be subordinated to value for life. Is his claim for the priority of value strong enough to stand if understood in this way?

Our supposition is a reasonable one. Given the failure of his attempt to reduce truth-claims to value-assessments, he must admit that when he opposes truth to value he is opposing things which are different in kind. The only alternative — to say that value-assessments derive their value from their *truth* — would undercut his assertion that a conception's value outweighs its truth. Thus, it is not available to him.

But if truth and value are considered to be different in kind, then one is confronted with a very sticky problem regarding the criterion to be used in deciding between them. One can hardly say, "A conception's value for life should be accorded preëminence in the decision of whether or not to adopt it because this is of greater value than the merely true," or "Since what has value for life may not be true, value for life should not be given precedence in the belief-adoption process." It is patent that to argue in either way would beg the question of the relative importance of truth and value. But what *tertium quid* could be found which might properly serve as a criterion for ranking them?

This is a difficult question indeed, and I think that the burden of answering it falls squarely on Nietzsche. This is because the burden of proof (of superiority, not of truth) is his. Since the beginning, truth has been considered to be the ultimate criterion of claims made before reason's tribunal. Thus, when Nietzsche declares that our first allegiance should be to value for life and not to truth, the onus is on him to show this. The reason for this is *not* that truth has always served us well (perhaps better than we have served it). To try to vindicate truth by an appeal to its value would be self-defeating in this context. The reason is that it devolves on him who proposes an innovation, especially one so radical, to show its superiority to the status quo. (I trust that I am not merely prostrating myself before *nomos* by saying this.) But this Nietzsche has not done, nor is it easy to see how he could do it in a non-question-begging way. As a result, his claim that a conception's value should carry more weight with us than its truth, although of course not refuted — indeed, to dismiss it because it were refuted would pre-suppose that truth were the court of last appeal — is nonetheless *unestablished*. The superiority of value to truth has not been shown by the use of a criterion which would have a fair claim to range over both of them.

130

To discover such a criterion — let us call it the *Hauptkriterium* — would be far from easy if only because its fitness to judge both truth and value would have to be granted as an axiom by the partisans of each. Otherwise, the partisans of truth would demand a *true* account of the *Hauptkriterium*'s fitness, and those of the value for life would require a demonstration of the value for life inherent in using it. And consider: if, *mirabile dictu*, such a criterion were found, then *it* and not truth or value would be the most fundamental criterion for belief-adoption.

In sum: Nietzsche can hardly expect us to acquiesce in his eminently controversial assertion of the primacy of value over truth without demonstrating value's superiority with reference to a criterion of the sort described above. But then this *Hauptkriterium* must be admitted to be more fundamental than either truth or value. Thus, Nietzsche cannot show value for life to be superior to truth without relegating both to an inferior rank.

But all of this is hypothetical. Nietzsche advances no *Hauptkriterium*, and he offers no demonstration — only the assertion — of the superiority of value for life to truth. His burden of proof is undischarged.

As a result, one has every right to tax Nietzsche with *lèse majesté* towards the truth. If nothing else, this robs him of a possible justification for his constant focus on Christianity's value. Had he been able to show that a conception's value is of more importance than its truth, he would have shown that his emphasis was the proper one. But as things stand, neither has been shown.

Finally, we might stop to consider in passing whether Nietzsche's claim for value against truth is properly a *philosophical* claim at all. One could well argue that philosophy, as a *practice*, has always aimed first and foremost at the truth of things and that this aim is part of what constitutes it. Thus if Nietzsche is aiming first and foremost at something else, viz., value-assessment, is he, properly speaking, engaged in philosophy at all? Compare this with the practice of medicine. Once granted that it aims primarily at the welfare of its patients, would we not say that one who aimed, not at their welfare, but at "enhancing life" by getting rid of them was not a bad physician but no physician at all? Many contemporary philosophers have been a bit anxious to see if Nietzsche has a union card. Perhaps they are right, if only on account of his views on truth.

In fine, one cannot excuse Nietzsche's nearly total neglect of the case *for* Christianity by saying that he had routed it with a counter-proof. The superiority of his own ideal for man, though arguable, is unestablished; even if it were granted as an axiom, it is a moot point as to whether and to what extent Christianity actually thwarts its attainment; there are severe empirical short-comings in his natural history of morals; and his atheism, a virtual *parti pris*, effectively begs the question against Christian theism. Nor has he excused this neglect by showing that a conception's value rather than its truth deserves one's chief attention. Nietzsche, who harangues the reader often and at length on Christianity's disvalue but accords short shrift to its pretensions to historical and metaphysical truth, has in effect marshalled the bulk of his forces against a lizard while a dragon waits unengaged in the rear. All in all, it is hard not to say of him something like what Mill said of Sedgwick and his objections to utilitarianism, especially if we bear in mind that for Mill "consequences" includes effects upon the character.

What he says against its truth, when picked out from a hundred different places, and brought together, would fill about three pages, leaving about twenty consisting of attacks upon its tendency. This already looks ill . . . [for] One thing is certain; that if an opinion have ever such mischievous consequences, that cannot prevent any thinking person from believing it, if the evidence is in its favour. . . . When, therefore, we find that this mode of dealing with an opinion is the favourite one — is resorted to in preference to the other, and with greater vehemence, and at greater length — we conclude that it is upon unthinking rather than upon thinking persons that the author calculates upon making an impression; or else, that he himself is one of the former class of persons — that his own judgment is determined, less by evidence presented to his understanding, than by the repugnancy of the opposite opinion to his partialities and affections; and that, perceiving clearly the opinion to be one which it would be painful for him to adopt, he has been easily satisfied with reasons for rejecting it.[25]

Despite all that we learn from Nietzsche, and it is much, the great part of the injuries and anathemas he rains down on *der Gekreuzigten* must seem, to a neutral party as well as to a believer, rather beside the point. Despite all, it might still be the case that the *Logos* says what is. And if it does, can its value be very problematic? For, to paraphrase Mill, if to know authentically in what order of things, under what government of the universe it is our destiny to live were not valuable, it is difficult to imagine what could be of value.[26]

CHAPTER FIVE

IN CONCLUSION

After a sketch of the ways in which the great philosophers have commonly stood in relation to their predecessors, this chapter proceeds to a final appraisal of Nietzsche's handling of Pascal and to a consideration of Nietzsche from a rather neglected perspective, the zoological.

If philosophy were, as Husserl once claimed, "rigorous science" (*strenge Wissenschaft*), we should expect most philosophers, if they are candid, to echo Newton's remark that he was able to see as far as he did because he stood on the shoulders of giants. But although Schopenhauer might make that claim with respect to Kant, or Aquinas to Aristotle or Spinoza to Descartes, this is not the usual relation of philosophers to their predecessors.

Viewed in a general way, the history of philosophy resembles Heinrich Schliemann's Troy site: layers of cities built atop the ruins of other, older cities, long-buried cities that an upheaval of the earth or an enterprising excavator might bring to the surface where, as they are no longer very habitable, they are not so much lived in as studied and admired. Or, from the perspective of the *laudator temporis acti*, the history of philosophy, surveyed from the present, might resemble nothing so much as medieval Rome: a small city long sunk from Imperial grandeur, a burg of near-rustic squalor, largely jerry-built from odds and ends plundered from the monuments of a dimly understood and little appreciated past, with pigs rooting where Caesars once had trod.

For my part, I think that philosophy in its sometimes random career has been mostly impelled by what André Gide called *les influences par réaction*. In other words, in philosophy action has been largely reaction. If it were not extravagant and rather absurd, I would say that the advance of philosophy resembles that of an astronaut in and about his ship in the weightlessness of space. In the zero-gravity of free thought, the philosopher finds that he can best progress by pushing against some massy, fixed object. It is a tricky business; the inexperienced spin themselves about every which way, rebounding almost at hazard and wildly pushing at objects which turn out not to be fixed after all.

On a more pedestrian level, precisely what are these *influences par réaction*?

They can be as mundane and collegial as problem-setting. The master, having taught his pupils all he knows, leaves them a problem as a farewell gift, perhaps inadvertently. So Porphyry, in an offhand comment on Aristotle's *Categories*, set the medievals the problem of universals; and so Descartes, by questioning the existence of any extra-mental reality, bequeathed the Realism/ Idealism problem to his successors down to the present day.

They may be obstacles blocking the philosopher's intended path like the boulder athwart Hannibal's Alpine pass, obstructions which must be surmounted or destroyed. So was Plato with his Forms and familial polity to Aristotle, and so was Parmenides with his doctrine of non-being to Plato in the *Sophist*. Then, despite his regard for his great forebear, the philosopher must "lay hands on father Parmenides," as Plato did, or simply shrug his shoulders in the Aristotelian manner and confess that truth is a greater friend than Plato. And it was in this spirit that Schopenhauer savaged the ethics of Kant, for whom he had the utmost esteem, so that he might clear the way for his own. Like Plato's Euthyphro, the philosopher does not scruple to prosecute his father for wrongdoing — or even (oh nadir of impiety!) to "lay hands on father Parmenides." Even Aristotle, long revered as The Philosopher and "*Il maestro di color che sanno*" (Dante's phrase), saw his turn come at last.

Finally, *les influences par réaction* may be understood as provocations or evocations. The sheer wanton perversity of error extorts the truth from us by way of response; we see in the wrong road a sign-post to the right one. We learn by *contradicting*: "It is not thus, but *thus*!" The stimulus of dialogue with the great dead whom the philosopher honors by electing as his opponents evokes, by way of response, thoughts that would not have arisen from ponderous soliloquizing. As Socrates saw, there is midwifery in dialectic.

No one exemplifies this dialectical process better than Nietzsche. From Schopenhauer he took Will as a provocation to pessimism and transformed it into something calling for the highest affirmations. Schopenhauer's morality of compassion became in his hands a war against pity. Pascal's asceticism and religiosity showed him health by showing him disease. Plato's world of Forms sent him running to champion the world of becoming, and Christianity — on his view the greatest No! ever said to the world — called forth its greatest Yes! from him. It would be no disparagement of Nietzsche to say that he, like many other philosophers, was first and foremost indebted to the "errors" of his predecessors.

Of course, it is one thing to allege that your esteemed forebears have erred, and another to show it. Did Nietzsche deal fairly with Pascal and his "errors"?

There would be little point in reproaching Nietzsche for not having read Pascal more carefully. True, had he read even Filleau's *Discours* or Étienne's *Préface* he might have had a more adequate idea of Pascal's over-all argument and responded accordingly. But great thinkers are often a bit casual in their dealings with their predecessors. Aristotle, as is well known, commonly represents the doctrines of earlier thinkers in terms peculiar to his own philosophy. Hegel also comes to mind as a man who, whatever his merits as a philosopher (I incline to Schopenhauer's estimate), is less than completely reliable when it comes to expositing the views of previous sages. And although we cannot be sure, it may well be, as Nietzsche said (J 190), that the Platonic Socrates is really "Plato in front, Plato behind and chimaera in the middle." To a certain extent, these liberties may be a result of the greatness of the mind that takes them. Perhaps one cannot know very many of one's predecessors *au fond* without having read one's mind to ruin, for reading – as Nietzsche reminds us (EH II 8) – can be an obstacle to independent thought and is certainly mind-numbing in excess. And perhaps a really powerful and original mind can scarcely avoid foisting its own, highly individual interpretation on the text of the past. Indeed, this process may be all to the good if it is not misunderstood by careless readers. Even the greatest authors do not know all of their own riches. Pascal saw himself as an apologist, a bulwark of orthodoxy; Nietzsche did not see him so, but he found in him what others had not seen. And if, say, the pedestrian Socrates of Xenophon is a fair copy of the historical son of Sophroniscus, then we are much the richer for Plato's invention of *his* Socrates.

Some might wish to reproach Nietzsche for often addressing to his predecessors and his public what amount to argument-sketches or even hints rather than full-blown arguments at key times. Strange though it may sound to some, this is less a matter of philosophical substance than style of philosophizing. One cannot write a treatise on behalf of every point to be made, and anyway, one may expect one's readers to make a modest contribution to the discussion. This practice shows respect for one's public and a grasp of rhetorical niceties, for, as Aristotle noted, in general enthymemes please more than syllogisms and are more persuasive. Nietzsche's readers should be very pleased and persuaded indeed.

It would be fair to fault him, though, for regarding truth too lightly in theory and in practice. Why did he do this?

In all likelihood he felt that he was only recognizing the consequences of his doctrine that "all is false" in the correspondence sense, that the world as such is unknowable. This doctrine, which seems to show the influence of Kant, must result in complete skepticism on the part of him who affirms it and yet wants to know the truth about the world. Perhaps this is what led Nietzsche to question the value of the will to truth. Why will the unattainable? Rather, why not will what is attainable and what we have always been affirming as "true" anyway, namely, what is life-promoting?[1]

This does not seem unreasonable granted that truth in the correspondence sense is in principle unattainable. This could even be used to replace the support Nietzsche offered for his pragmatic theory of truth in FW 110 and 111, i.e., an account of the truth-making process that would have to be true in the correspondence sense. One can simply say that "ought" implies "can." Thus, there is no reason to strive for unattainable truth-about-the-world, and so we ought to settle for calling what is life-promoting "true."

Of course, whether or not truth in the correspondence sense is really unattainable is a very vexed question. I have taken Nietzsche's assertion of its impossibility to be based on Kantian grounds if on anything, although I do not think it necessarily follows from them.[2]

But if Nietzsche's regard for truth is sometimes too slender, so, too often, is that of the "commonplace Christian" whom he censures on the same grounds (MA I 116). This charge dates back to the earliest days of the Christian era — one recalls that Galen, Celsus and Porphyry were also shocked at the Christians' reliance on hearsay, mere assertion for proof.[3] Also, there has been and is a tendency for believers to assume that the positive effects of belief are a sign of its truth, and inevitably gullibility and superstition have played a part in some cases as well. But, obviously, the conferring of peace of soul is, alas, no more a sure hallmark of truth than Descartes' "clearness and distinctness" or the Stoics' *kriterion*. And one need not be a W.K. Clifford to see a total reliance on mere hearsay, even if learned at or over one's mother's knee, as betokening a certain want of mental hygiene. But these are virtual platitudes.

Needless to say, however, not all Christians are "commonplace" in the respect just mentioned. Pascal, for example, was singularly determined to ferret out the truth concerning Christian belief. This is true of him despite his faith; despite his views on reason's frailty; despite his conviction that belief reached through inspiration, through the heart is not only legitimate (#110) but necessary for salvation (#808); and despite his passionate longing that

140

reasoning might be dispensed with, an indication perhaps of his fear of error in a game where the stakes are so high.

> As if reason were the only way we could learn! Would to God, on the contrary, that we never needed it and knew everything by instinct and feeling! But nature has refused us this blessing, and has instead given us only very little knowledge of this kind. . . .   (#110)

All of this notwithstanding, Pascal does strive mightily with his reason to unmask the truth. Nor does he do this only out of the rhetorical necessity of meeting the *libertin* on common ground. Nietzsche was right, I think, when he said that Pascal spoke loudly to reassure *himself* as well (M 91). Despite the searing *nuit de feu*, despite the meticulous observance of religious practices which, on his account of habit ("the machine"), should have made religion second nature to him, Pascal was not immune to doubt.

> I look around in every direction and all I see is darkness. Nature has nothing to offer me that does not give rise to doubt and anxiety. If I saw no sign there of a Divinity I should decide on a negative solution; if I saw signs of a Creator everywhere I should peacefully settle down in the faith. But, seeing too much to deny and not enough to affirm, I am in a pitiful state, where I have wished a hundred times over that, if there is a God supporting nature, she should unequivocally proclaim him, and that, if the signs in nature are deceptive, they should be completely erased; that nature should say all or nothing so that I could see what course I ought to follow. Instead of that, in the state in which I am, not knowing what I am nor what I ought to do, I know neither my condition nor my duty. My whole heart strains to know what the true good is in order to pursue it: no price would be too high to pay for eternity.
>
> I envy those of the faithful whom I see living so unconcernedly, making so little use of a gift which, it seems to me, I should turn to such different account.[4]   (#429)

141

One would naturally expect that Pascal, a Christian, would be decidedly dogmatic and that Nietzsche, an atheist and *libre-penseur*, would be supremely undogmatic. But to a considerable extent the reverse is true, for unlike Nietzsche's disbelief Pascal's faith is far from a *parti pris*. Pascal is honest; he admits that the matters in question are surpassingly difficult, that the case for Christianity is strong but by no means conclusive, and that nothing could prove it utterly short of the lightnings of the last day. As a result, he feels profound compassion for those who seek the truth without finding any answer, let alone his. By comparison, Nietzsche's sweeping, almost cavalier certainties sometimes seem rash and premature.

Philosophy as Exotic Zoology

In closing, I should like to consider Nietzsche in one of the ways he considered Pascal and others, as a *specimen* of the twists, turns, varieties and multiplicities which can inform the human spirit.

This procedure may seem objectionable in principle. After all, was it not a defect in Nietzsche's *modus operandi* that he had continuously before him Pascal the man, "the most instructive victim of Christianity," and slighted what made this remarkable man so remarkable, his ideas, by treating them as mere symptoms?

There is force to this objection, but this should not blind us to the merits of adopting the perspective in question on occasion.

Philosophy, as Nietzsche intuitively saw, can be construed as a kind of exotic zoology.[5] For, taken by and large, the great philosophers are curious types indeed. It is important to discover that such men existed since one would never have been able to imagine them on one's own.[6] It is important for more than merely voyeuristic reasons of the sort which once impelled visitors to London to put Bedlam on their itinerary. And it is important not only as a contribution to empirical psychology. It is, above all, important to philosophy as traditionally understood, philosophy as expressed in the Delphic and Socratic injunction "Know thyself." To know what we are involves knowing what we are capable of being, our potency as well as our present act. And it involves knowing ourselves not only as individuals but as members of a species. We come to know the limits of the plasticity of our common human nature by coming to know the wealth of types our species has produced, and in the welter of these types the philosopher is at once one of the noblest and most exotic, a fit object of admiration and perhaps aspiration. For example, whether Spinoza's system is true or false in the main, I am interested to know that there was a man who could conceive of all phenomena, even the most disparate, as features of a vast unity and find that one Substance divine. Whether or not Diogenes of Sinope was correct in what little he put forward as doctrine, I am glad to learn that at least one philosopher thought philosophy bid him surpass his fellows in right living as well as in cognition. When I read Parmenides I am impressed, not by the soundness of his reasoning, but by his unflagging willingness to follow his reason wherever it may lead, even to conclusions the whole world would rate as mad. Descartes' foundations for human knowledge may wobble, but I am deepened by learning that a man lived who thought that what all regard as evident was in dire need, not only of foundations, but of the strongest possible ones. In discovering these men we learn what kind of thing man is, and as man is the kind of thing we are, we discover ourselves specifically. This is part of what underlies Terence's celebrated *"Homo sum, et nihil humani a me alienum puto."*[7]

What, then, is to be found in the man Nietzsche? First let me say what I do not find.

I do not see in him what Jaspers saw, that is, a naturally Christian soul. Jaspers says that "Nietzsche, the pastor's son, knew and admitted the Christian basis of his real motivating forces: his seriousness, truthfulnesss and radically uncompromising approach."[8] But these semblances of common ground are illusory or superficial. Nietzsche and the Christian are radically uncompromising in espousing contrary doctrines, a fact which far outweighs any shared zeal. Nietzsche was so far from seeing seriousness as one of his principal motive forces that he called his teaching *"la gaya scienza,"* and his Zarathustra says: "And when I beheld my devil, I found him serious, thorough, profound, solemn: it was the Spirit of Gravity — through him all things are ruined" (Z I 7). And we have seen that his commitment to truth had its theoretical and practical limits.

When I look at Nietzsche, I see, as have so many others, a man neither at one with himself nor with his work. He may be right in seeing a tragedy in Pascal's warfare against the self and the senses, but his own conflicts make his case scarcely less tragic. Each had civil war in him, to use a figure of Pascal's.

An apostle of strength and health, Nietzsche was chronically ill, suffering from tremendous headaches. And the man who claimed to stand on a height and search out the secrets of the all-too-human far below was acutely myopic. He wanted but was unable to secure sympathetic female companionship; twice his offers of marriage were turned down. A nondescript man who preached greatness but passed virtually unnoticed among his contemporaries, he spent most of his life among the very people he excoriated in his writings – commonplace Christians, very ordinary folk, "the insipid European herd animal of today." He proclaimed an unquenchable passion for truth though he sometimes slighted truth. In part this was a result of his obsession with value, but in addition to this he seems sometimes to have gotten a bit carried away and to have waxed too hyperbolic; spoken too stridently, strived too much for *effect* – as when, transported no doubt by a desire to put distance between himself and the Germans, he falsely boasted descent from Polish noblemen (EH I 3). Kung is right, I think, when he says that there is something of the actor in the grand manner in Nietzsche.[9]

But most importantly, he trades in what he declares to be contraband, for he anathematizes religion while lapsing into its forms. He has his own dogmas, the faith of a faithless man – God is dead, the beyond is a fable, power is good. He has his own evangel – that of the Overman, and like some latter-day John the Baptist he would make straight his way. Moreover, his attempt to establish the Eternal Return as a physical theory (WM 1053– 1067) shows an undeniable and unfulfilled craving to endow the here and now with a significance beyond itself. When one couples these things with the madness of his last years, it is hard not to feel that, despite his striking brilliance, he is so little of a piece as to be more than a little *manqué*. Seen from a certain perspective – the Pascalian, for example – the contradictions in and between his life and thought might make him "the most instructive victim" of the resolve to understand the world solely in immanent terms.

The fact that Nietzsche did feel compelled to understand the world solely in immanent terms reveals the very heart of the difference between him and Pascal, and more than anything it makes me wonder if Pascal's blood really did run in Nietzsche's veins.

Nietzsche was afflicted with a kind of metaphysical myopia. I do not mean that he failed to see that there was such a thing as metaphysical reality; I mean that he was never able to see the existence of transcendent reality as even a bare possibility. He simply rejected metaphysics out of hand, and with it "God," "soul," "beyond" and so on. "In the ages of crude primeval culture," he blandly declared, "man believed that in dreams he got to know *another, real world*: here is the origin of all metaphysics" (MA I 5). Augustine tells us in the *Confessions* that his inability to conceive of immaterial substance long prevented him from becoming a Christian, and that it was his acquaintance with Platonism which finally enabled him to grasp it as possible (V 19, 25; VII 26). Nietzsche never made this step. He lacked the imagination, if that is the word, to see metaphysics or Christianity "from the inside," even if only for the purpose of playing the devil's advocate.[10]

One can hardly fault Nietzsche for not seeing what, in all honesty, it seems that he just could not see. And yet, without prejudging the issue of whether or not there is any transcendent reality that the mind might grasp, I would say that a man like Nietzsche is deficient in a way that a man like Pascal is not. Pascal was alive in a way that few men have ever been to the possibility of a world behind this one, a reality beyond the physical. There can be little doubt that such a sensitivity is an advantage to the philosopher. Of course, it might lead him far astray, deep into a never-never land of brain-webs wrought of words without reference or even sense. But it gives him access to a realm which, if it is not of such stuff as dreams are made on, just might be the

146

place where the final truths about things dwell. Only one with a sensitivity, an openness like Pascal's can tell, for only he can look there.

APPENDIX

LOOSE LEAVES FROM THE COMMONPLACE
BOOK OF A SKEPTICAL FIDEIST

To be a philosophical skeptic is, in
a man of letters, the first and most
essential step towards being a sound,
believing Christian.

Hume, *Dialogues Concerning
Natural Religion*

It is to no end surprising that scoffers should persist in the attempt, of necessity vain, to refute Christian belief by alleging contradictions between it and what we "know" to be true of the world or compatible with divinity. As if such thrusts could not be blunted by the most inexpert defender! And as if Christian Scriptures, theology and apologetics were not a mine of far more damaging objections! Indeed, neither philological attacks on Scripture in the manner begun by Porphyry, nor the sobering historical fact that Christianity burgeoned as a blind faith in an era of unsurpassed credulity is apt to be so damaging.[1]

It is all very well to claim that the existence of an omnipotent, omniscient, wholly benevolent deity is incompatible with the metaphysical, moral and physical evil that the sorry scheme of things entire does in fact contain — that such a being would wish to abolish evil, would know how to and would be able to, and hence if he existed evil would not.[2] And it is all very well to thunder *"Deus, quem Paulus creavit, dei negatio"*[3] — that divinity is incompatible with espousal of a morality such as the Christian, that no deity could be both benevolent and hidden, and so forth. From a logical point of view, these arguments are decisive: no being *such as they describe* could exist save, *per impossibile*, as a contradiction in terms.

However, if there is a personal being who is *summum ens*, it need not be the case that he should happen to conform *in detail* to the descriptions of "God" in the above-mentioned arguments. Those arguments prove, not that there is no God, but only that there is no being possessed of attributes identical to those presumed in the arguments.[4] Thus, the Christian apologist need only aver that what he worships as the God of Abraham, Isaac and Jacob differs in some respect from the "God" of the scoffers' atheistical ratiocinations. He can take the drastic step of denying that the God he worships has a certain attribute at all,[5] or the more modest one of granting the possession of the attribute in name but insisting that the attribute be redefined.[6]

From a rhetorical point of view, the weakness of such attempts at a refutation of God's existence resides in the fact that they assume premises (e.g., a certain definition of "God" or of a divine attribute) that the theist, if cornered, can refuse to grant. A much stronger case against Christian theism can be made if one proceeds from premises to which the believer is committed *de fide* and which he holds to be essential components of his creed. If a contradiction is generated from these assumptions, then, as we shall see, the believer's options are much more limited.

In short, one who would confute Christianity is best advised to limit himself to internal, i.e., intra-framework objections. He should argue from principles found in the Christian's Scriptures, creeds and theology. In other words, "Look to the fable."

Probably the most famous of these intra-framework objections are the incompatible genealogies of Jesus (Math. 1:1–16 and Luke 3:23–28) and Jesus' unfulfilled prophecy that the Second Coming would occur in the days of the then present generation (Math. 24:34–35). But far more fundamental are the objections, hoary but still potent, of the immorality of God and the apparent contra-rationality of the Christian Mysteries. Christian belief can, with difficulty, withstand these objections, but the price of avoiding refutation is not small.

It is a commonplace among scoffers that the Christian God, especially as depicted in the Old Testament, is distressingly anthropomorphic, and, worse, is often in flagrant violation of his own moral precepts.[7] To take only one example, Yahweh includes "Thou shalt not kill" in the Decalogue and is quite detailed in his prescription for penalties for homicide in Deuteronomy, but his own conduct in this regard is far from exemplary. Leaving aside that he tries (and fails) to kill Moses (Ex. 4:24), that he kills the Amorites with huge hailstones and prolongs the day over Gibeon so that Joshua may make a more thorough slaughter (Jos. 10:11–15), consider only his war instructions to the Israelites. In far off towns they are to slay all the menfolk, but they may keep the women, children and livestock as booty. But in the towns which they are given by Yahweh as their inheritance, they are commanded to "save alive nothing that breatheth." The fruit trees in the plain, however, they are ordered to spare (Deut. 20: 10–20).[8]

Christian apologists from the earliest times to the present have considered rival religions to be refuted that worshipped divinities of questionable morals. Clement, Tertullian, Augustine and many others are eloquent on the foibles of the gods of classical antiquity.[9] Zeus is an adulterer; Hermes a thief; Hera vindictive; and Aphrodite a slut. The pagans should realize — nay, should already have realized — that the beings they worship could not be gods. Indeed, they could only be demons! Pascal holds it against Islam that Mahomet slew whereas Jesus did not (209). And C.S. Lewis, converted in good Pascalian fashion first to simple theism and then to Christianity, decided against Hinduism on the basis of the immorality licensed by its gods.[10] In short, Christians have always been willing to indict the gods of other sects on various moral grounds. They have alleged that plainly immoral behavior is flat-out incompatible with divinity. Why is not *their* God hoist with that very same petard?

This astoundingly naive objection can be countered, but only at the cost of hamstringing Christians' apologetic efforts to refute rival faiths.

The usual response to it is that passages in the Christian Scriptures which seem to speak unworthily of God must not be construed literally but *sensu allegorico*. This is how Augustine's difficulties with the Old Testament, long a stumbling block to his acceptance of Catholicism, were resolved by St. Ambrose.[11] But why may not rival religions avail themselves of this procedure? Why may not they say that the apparent grossness of their fables is but a cover for a deeper, more elevated and spiritual meaning? It would be methodological bad faith to say that potential counter-evidence in one's own sacred texts may be defused by figurative interpretation while difficulties in the texts and traditions of rivals must be understood *ad litteram*.[12]

Of course, instead of interpreting offending passages as figures or as well nigh inevitable distortions of godhead resulting from the concrete historical circumstances of a Scripture's human author(s) — options, to repeat, which are open to anyone of any creed — one can simply insist on the utter inscrutability of transcendent godhood. Who are we, things of a day, to judge of Him? "Where wast thou when I laid the foundations of the earth?" (Job 38:4) Or, as the Eagle said to Dante in the *Paradiso*, "Who are you to take the judgment seat, and pass on things a thousand miles away, who cannot see the ground before your feet? . . . O earthbound animals! O gross minds!" (XIX 79, Ciardi's version). On this view, we can only have faith that God's will and acts are holy and just, little though they may seem so to us on occasion. Perhaps Abraham, when Yahweh bid him sacrifice his son on a mountain in Moriah, did not see how the deed might be fitting and right. Yet he had faith and lifted the knife. As Kierkegaard says of him, "He believed and did not doubt, he believed the preposterous."[13] And our task is to do likewise, one may affirm.

This is sublime, but there are difficulties.

The first and most obvious is that the believer is still in the dilemma of having to admit that his own faith is refuted or of having to admit that the moral indictments of other faiths' deities by his co-religionists are indecisive. Others too may take refuge in the majesty and inscrutability of godhood.

But the second and more important is that the believer has put himself on a very slippery and very dangerous slope, for in effect he has declared that nothing will count as a refutation of his faith.[14]

Suppose that your deity bids you sacrifice your son but no ram comes out of the bushes at the last moment? Suppose that you are bid to murder travellers, as the Thugs thought themselves bid by Kali? Suppose you are told to cast certain of your children into a flaming furnace, as Moloch's worshippers were told. Will your faith sustain you always in like passes? If it will, then you are a man who is capable of anything so long as it is "divinely bid." If you categorically declare yourself to be incompetent to judge of God, then no matter what you are ostensibly bid or told by him you must never conclude that you converse, not with divinity, but with spirit of another sort. You must never conclude that a ventriloquist is hidden near the sacred tripod, or that the Pythian priestess is an insane or malevolent sham, no matter how unworthy the "divine utterance" may appear. The faith of Abraham, sublime and total, is irrefutable, but if it is misplaced he will never — can never — learn his error. The faith of Abraham is sublime, but when it has been wrong it has wrought innumerable sectarian outrages and cultist barbarities. And it has ensured that Voltaire prophesied correctly when he said that "*Tantum religio potuit suadere malorum*"[15] was a line that would live as long as the world.

More threatening than morals to the security of Christian belief is the patently contra-rational character of the Mysteries of orthodox theology. They have traditionally been held to be essential constituents of Christian faith, but they are contra-rational insofar as they appear to be either internally inconsistent or at odds with what reason declares self-evident. A few examples:[16]

1) It is *de fide* that The Father is God, The Son is God and the Holy Spirit is God. It is also an article of faith that 'God' is the name of one thing, an individual, and not the name of a species. Thus the 'is' in 'The Father is God,' etc., asserts identity and not mere predication. But this implies that the Three Persons are identical to one another (since things identical to the same thing must be identical to each other) as well as tritheism. However, orthodox theology denies both conclusions.

2) According to the Nicene Creed, the Second Person of the Trinity, the Son, is "begotten of" the First, the Father. Yet it is denied that the Second Person's being is derivative from or dependent on that of the First. Yet 'y is begotten of x' implies, in any nonequivocal sense of 'is begotten of,' that y depends on x for its existence.[17]

3) God is credited with having made the universe *ex nihilo*, whereas it is self-evident that nothing can be made out of nothing.

Objections of this sort have been out of fashion since the days of Pierre Bayle and his skeptical successors in the Enlightenment. But surely to affirm as the highest truths, not only mere implausibilities such as miracles, but patent contradictions and absurdities, would confute a faith if anything could. The Mysteries are made-to-order objections to Christian belief, and the Christian needs to respond with much more than a shrug of the shoulders and a traditional *"Mysterium, non mendacium est."*[18] How can he respond?

I   The believer can of course simply break with orthodoxy and revise the Mysteries so as to make them compatible with reason,[19] but this involves a heavy cost. Not only would he be compelled to admit that God has allowed himself to be seriously misunderstood by the vast majority of believers — a neglect which would bespeak scant solicitude on the part of one held to be benevolence itself — but insofar as the doctrines in question are essential constituents of Christian belief, the revising believer would be abandoning Christianity for something else under that name. Of course Christianity as traditionally taught and understood, the "faith of our fathers," can, as can any theory, avoid refutation by changing form like Proteus during the wrestling match. But this is escaping through perishing, defense by surrender, even if in the long run it should be the most attractive option.

II   Needless to say, the Christian may try to show that any contradictions in orthodox theology are only apparent, resulting either from faulty reasoning (this is Aquinas' view in *SCG* I 7) or from a misprision regarding what is actually affirmed. And he may say that this road has already been travelled to its end, that philosophers and theologians such as the great Scholastics have succeeded in showing the Christian Mysteries to be self-consistent, mutually compatible and unopposed to self-evidence.

Without examining all of the proposed solutions in detail — a task for a far more detailed and ambitious work — the following provisional observations may be made.

First of all, it would appear that one has every right to be skeptical of any attempt at giving consistent elucidations of the Mysteries as being *in principle* foredoomed to failure. How could *any* argumentation show that what is patently contradictory is, after all, not contradictory? What patience would we have with a man who said we ought not to pronounce square circles to be impossible because sufficient acuity could discern harmony between the apparently jarring predicates? Would we not — rightly — rule out the possibility of such a solution *a priori*?

Secondly, the presumption against the worth of any proposed consistent elucidations of the Mysteries is increased by even the most cursory glance at the liberties philosophers have allowed themselves in such attempts. Aquinas, for example, concludes that the Persons of the Trinity are "subsistent relations" (*ST* 1a 29, 4). How could a relation possibly be subsistent? What could it mean to be a *"relationem ut subsistentem"* as opposed to a relation as an accident? Clearly, one mystery has been explained by another.

In fine, the presumption is entirely against the very possibility of explaining the Mysteries consistently.

III   The believer can bite the proverbial bullet and say, as philosophers such as Descartes have done, that God is not bound by the principle of non-contradiction, that what is impossible for man is not so for God, and thus that God may so devise things that contradictory doctrines are yet true.

This solution is scarcely less troublesome than the problem. In effect it is utter fideism of Abraham's kind, abject insistence on the utter inscrutability of godhood, and thus it removes the discussion from the rational realm altogether. It is, moreover, decidely *ad hoc*, for the attribution to God of exemption from the law of non-contradiction seems designed only to save him from refutation. In addition, it is a tool that rival religionists can avail themselves of when confronted with the critiques of the Christians: one's rivals too can say that, by the grace of god, the inconsistencies in their fables are true and constitute no objection. And needless to say, the affirmation of contradictions in one's conceptual scheme has consequences that go far beyond apologetics, for by the Law of Duns Scotus not only the Mysteries but *everything*, all propositions and their negations, would be "proved." To set God above the principle of non-contradiction will prove too much.

IV   Finally, the Christian might say, not that he believes contradictions in the traditional accounts of God to be true or to have been shown to be merely apparent, but that these contradictions are in principle resolvable even if not by us at this or any other time. For he could claim, as Bayle did, that although in isolation the Mysteries might seem to be objectionable, once it is realized that God bids us believe them, all difficulties should vanish.[20] That is, we have God's word that what from our perspective is irrational is truth from his.

But here too objections abound. Again, the reasoning seems decidedly *ad hoc* — its purpose is only to avert the overthrow of a favorite theory. And again, Christian critiques of rival faiths are hamstrung since rivals too can claim that contradictions in their fables are seen to be tractable when viewed by Deity *sub specie aeternitatis*. But, more importantly, this reasoning begs the question. In the context of an attempt to refute Christian belief by adducing the Mysteries as counter-evidence, the very existence of God is at issue and so his warrant for the Mysteries' ultimate intelligibility and rationality is inadmissible.

158

None of these options can be very attractive to the believer. The result of adopting number one is that if you are an orthodox Christian, the rational thing to do is to turn your back on millenia of tradition and become something rather different. Two presents the believer with a promissory note that looks as if it cannot, as a matter of principle, be paid. Three proves far too much, and the upshot of four is that it is marginally reasonable to be a Christian but not to become one. Moreover, all save number one seriously weaken traditional Christian polemics against rival faiths, and so they reinforce the difficulty consequent on four.

The Christian can better the situation, however, by invoking certain dread shades from the rationalists' underworld: the antinomies.

As all philosophers know, the antinomies are valid deductions of contradictory conclusions from premises whose truth appears self-evident. They have been discovered in set theory and semantics,[21] and of course Kant in the *Critique of Pure Reason* sees them in metaphysics. As their name implies, they "oppose the law" of logic that truth is preserved by valid inference from true premises. Logic declares the antinomies to be impossible notwithstanding that they have the effrontery to be, or to appear to be, actual.

What is the lesson of the antinomies?

The manner of their proper resolution(s), if any, is very much an open question.[22] We simply do not know just how to deal with them. The types of possible solution are known, however, and any of them would lend some help to the Christian theist in the sorry pass described above. Whether the help is very great is another matter.

If the antinomy is an unsound argument, then one or both of the following possibilities must be actual.

a) The antinomy proceeds from one or more false premises. — As the premises of antinomies appear to be self-evidently true, this would prove that we can be mistaken about even vivid self-evidence, that self-evidence may be only apparent and yet withstand close inspection by fine minds over many years.

b) The reasoning of the antinomy is invalid. — Although the validity was established by a finite number of mechanical steps and the propriety of each was self-evident, nonetheless the self-evident propriety of one or more steps was only apparent, even if overwhemingly so.

If, strange to say, the antinomy is after all a sound argument, then, since its premises are true and its reasoning valid, it must have a true conclusion, and so one of the following must be true.

c) The conclusion is not self-contradictory. — Though its self-contradictory character may be self-evident, and perhaps demonstrable by a finite number of mechanical steps whose propriety, in each case, is self-evident, yet at some point or points the self-evidence was only apparent.

d) The conclusion is in fact self-contradictory, but it is true nonetheless since it was validly derived from true premises.

And finally, there is a description of the antinomy which does not seem to fit in either of the categories above. It is that the antinomy is just what it appears to be: an argument with true premises, valid reasoning and a false conclusion.

Of course, by orthodox logical standards only a) is a genuine possibility, but the force of the antinomies comes precisely from the fact that a) does not appear to be a problem: the premises of the antinomies appear to be quite in order. As a result, the antinomies challenge our logical standards very forcefully and constitute, until and if they are satisfactorily resolved, powerful grounds for skepticism regarding the scope and efficacy of reason. In the meantime, it is very much an open question as to which of the types of resolution is correct for a given antinomy, no matter how implausible or logically heterodox some of them may be. For the antinomies, by the mere fact of their existence, vociferously call into question the very foundations of our notions of sound reasoning.

We see, then, that the orthodox Christian can, if he wishes, evade the rationalist charge of believing the absurd and contradictory by challenging the assumption that rationality is a fixed, given, and unproblematic standard against which faith may be measured. For the canon of reason that declares faith wanting also declares that no argument can be what the antinomies have so far appeared to be — a valid inference from true premises yielding a contradictory conclusion.

Consequently, one accepting the Mysteries could argue that their self-evident falsity (*creation ex nihilo*) or self-evident contradictoriness (monotheism/tritheism) is not *utterly conclusive* against them since the complete reliability of self-evidence is, at present, an open question. And just as the antinomies may arise from false propositions which, from a phenomenological point of view, extort our assent, so the Mysteries may contain true propositions which, from a phenomenological point of view, extort our denial.[23]

Or he could say that, contrary to all expectation, self-contradictory statements might possibly be true since such statements follow, in the antinomies, from what just might be (as they appear to be) valid reasoning and true premises.

Or he might argue, with greater verisimilitude, that if reason oversteps its competence in dealing with sets and the semantics of natural language, it may equally well if not more likely do so when it seeks to come to grips with God.

In short, even though the Christian Mysteries, as traditionally expressed, are apparently contra-rational, the orthodox believer can answer objections on this score without having recourse to particular attempts to demonstrate their consistency. This is just as well since such attempts, apparently futile in principle, are highly chancy at best.

Also, the believer can respond to objections without merely affirming that from within the framework of Christian faith it is reasonable to believe the Mysteries on God's word. This reply deprived him of common ground with his opponents and so was rhetorically useless.

And finally, the believer can affirm the limits of reason, the speciousness of self-evidence, or the tractability or even truth of apparent contradictions and absurdities in a way that is not *ad hoc*. For he has now, in the antinomies, independent grounds for affirming that, contrary to rationalist dogma, the possibility of these things must be considered to be an open question.

Still, to be saved from refutation by invoking such tenuous possibilities results in a Pyrrhic victory at best. Arguments based on uncertainties in rationality have a way of not stopping where one wants them to. Any scoffer who wishes to can invoke the problematic status of self-evidence, etc., against the dogmatic structure of Christian theology itself. Christian critiques of rival faiths are vitiated, because no matter how absurd or inconsistent their fables may be, they can avail themselves of the same devices as the Christians to avoid refutation. And not only rival religionists can make use of such arguments. Anyone can who, like a doting parent with a child in whom he will see no fault, has a cherished theory which *must* be right, whose failings therefore can be *only* apparent. The Faith will stand impregnable, but what *could be* overthrown if contradictoriness and absurdity should cease to be *decisive* objections? And yet, the Christian skeptical fideist is within his rights to insist that they are *not necessarily* conclusive objections, for he has the evidence of the antinomies on his side.

The orthodox Christian has won this much: he has shown that his belief in the Mysteries is *not necessarily* irrational, that the problems the antinomies pose leave the *possibility* of the Mysteries' truth an open question. Thus, with some epistemological audacity, he has established a right to affirm his faith as being, for all we know, compatible with reason. The Mysteries need not drive him to misology.

Yet this victory was won only by dismantling old outworks and artillery and dropping their debris on the enemy where the battle was the thickest. Or, to indulge in another similitude, one might recall that in 375 the Romans allowed the Goths to cross the Danube because they needed Gothic arms to help defend their hard-pressed frontiers. A generation later the Goths sacked Rome.

I dare say, though, that history will not repeat itself. The orthodox, apparently anti-rational faith I have tried to defend has much declined in number of adherents, especially of late now that Christians have so rigidly subordinated doctrine and dogma to universal love and good works. There is scarcely anyone left in Rome to notice if it should be sacked, and it has so shrunk in wealth and glory that I doubt if barbarians would consider it worth the sacking. Almost all of the old Romans have moved off to Constantinople, which I am told is a city much easier to defend.

Philo Baylis
Rome. A.D. 1983. Easter

NOTES

1 Pascal, *Pensées*, #413, in *Oeuvres Complètes*, ed. by Louis Lafuma (Paris: Éditions du Seuil, 1963), hereafter referred to as OC. All subsequent references to the *Pensées* are to the numeration of this edition.

2 Jean Duvergier de Hauranne, called St. Cyran because he was head of the abbey of that name, was a collaborator of Cornelius Jansenius whose *Augustinus*, appearing posthumously in 1640, was the "Bible" of Jansenism. St. Cyran was a tireless proselytizer for the doctrines of Jansenius until his death in 1643. Antoine Arnauld, the next head of the Jansenists in France, was his disciple.

3 The most controversial aspect of Jansenist doctrine concerned the bestowal of grace. Roughly speaking, the Jansenists held that a) grace is a free gift of God bestowed on the elect, none of whom can properly be said to merit it because of their corruption consequent on the Fall of Adam, and b) this grace is efficacious; it cannot fail of its salutary effect. In short, for a man to be saved the man must will it and God must will it, but the man cannot will it unless God does. And if God does, he must. Pascal's *Lettres à un provincial* contain lucid and stimulating accounts of contemporary disputes over grace, and his *Écrits sur la grâce*, a most important work for the understanding of Pascal, is just as lucid and perhaps even more knowledgeable.

4 A list of his early accomplishments would include his widely acclaimed *Essai sur les coniques*, written when he was sixteen, and his invention of a calculating machine at nineteen. A mathematical prodigy, his attendance with his father at the meetings at Père Mersenne's brought him to the notice of the leading mathematicians of the day when he was only twelve. At that age he had, according to his sister Gilberte (*Vie de M. Pascal*, OC, p. 19), independently discoverd the first thirty-two propositions of Euclid. (This venerable story may well be true, but it has

met with surprisingly little skepticism given the markedly hagiographical bent of the *Vie*.)

5 P #913. Many have thought that Pascal passed those hours in the grip of some vision or mystical rapture. But according to Jean Steinmann, "L'examen de cet autographe [the Memorial] prouve que Pascal n'a eu aucune vision. On n'y trouve aucun dessin tremblé, aucun signe caractéristique d'une extase quelconque." *Les Trois Nuits de Pascal* (Paris: Desclée de Brouwer, 1962), p. 33. Perhaps.

6 G. Périer, *Vie de M. Pascal*, pp. 23–24 in OC.

7 I have, for clarity of exposition, used the term "*liasse*" rather loosely. Properly, of course, it means "bundle" but I have used it synonymously with "unity" taken in the sense of a material whole. A more precise usage would not extend "*liasse*" to all of the material unities designated by Roman numerals, some of which are composed only of a page or two. For an account of the material aspect of the unities I–XXXV see Jean Mesnard, *Les Pensées de Pascal* (Paris: SEDES, 1976), pp. 33–38. This magisterial work is indispensable to any serious student of the *Pensées*.

8 For good accounts of the discovery of additional *pensées* and for the history of the *Pensées* in general see Louis Lafuma's *Histoire des Pensées de Pascal* (Paris: Éditions du Luxembourg, 1954) and especially vol. I of Mesnard's Pascal, *Oeuvres Complètes* (Paris: Desclée de Brouwer, 1964). A good short account can be found in the appendices of Mesnard's *LPP*, pp. 362–370.

9 É. Périer, *Préface de l'édition de Port-Royal*, OC, p. 498.

10 *Ibid.* The other members of the committee were Étienne Périer, Pierre Nicole, Filleau de la Chaise, Goibaud du Bois, le comte de Brienne and Antoine Arnauld.

11 Antoine Arnauld, "Lettre à M. Périer," *Oeuvres de Messire Antoine Arnauld*, XLIII vols. (Lausanne: Sigismond d'Arnay et Compagnie, 1775; reissued by Culture et Civilisation, Brussells, 1964), vol. I, p. 642 (Lettre CCXXX).

12 These citations from Condorcet's *Pensées de Pascal, Nouvelle édition, commentée, corrigée et augmentée* (London: 1776) have been taken from Lafuma's *HPP*, pp. 47–48.

13 This text is cited by Lafuma, *HPP*, pp. 53–54; it is taken from Cousin's "Rapport à l'Académie Française sur la nécessité d'une nouvelle édition

des *Pensées* de Pascal," *Journal des Savants* (1842), pp. 243-252, 333–358, 406–426, 490–505, 532–553, 608–625, 678–691. Lafuma remarks of Cousin (*HPP*, p. 53), that inasmuch as he was a peer of France, a member of two academies, former Minister of Public Instruction and director of the prestigious École Normale, he had enough titles to make himself heard.

14 Cf. Léon Brunschvicg's "Introduction aux *Pensées* de Pascal" in vol. XII of *Oeuvres de Blaise Pascal*, ed. by Léon Brunschvicg, Pierre Boutroux and Félix Gazier, XIV vols. (Paris: Hachette, 1904–1921), pp. XLIII–XLVIII.

Two photocopy editions of the autograph material have been published. The first was Brunschvicg's *L'original des Pensées de Pascal. Facsimile du manuscrit 9202 (fonds français) de la Bibliothèque Nationale* (Paris: Hachette, 1905). The second was Lafuma's *Le Manuscrit des Pensées de Pascal* (Paris: Les Librairies Associés, 1962).

15 Cf. Lafuma, *HPP*, pp. 64–66. Michaut, like contemporary editors of the *Pensées*, wished to present the fragments in Pascal's final arrangement. This was a step in the right direction, but he did not realize that the *Recueil Original* preserved the order of 1710–1711 and not that of 1662.

16 Patricia Topliss, *The Rhetoric of Pascal* (Amsterdam: Leicester University Press, 1966), p. 157.

17 Cf. Lafuma, *HPP*, pp. 77–78. It was Tourneur who advanced the claim which Brunschvicg had entertained as a mere hypothetical, viz., that ms. 9203 reflects the order in which Pascal left his papers. He did not however seem entirely confident of his thesis. It was left to Lafuma to argue for it in a manner which would convince the learned public. See *Mercure de France*, December 1947 and January 1948, and "Pascal a-t-il classé ses papiers?" in *Recherches pascaliennes* (Paris: Delmas, 1949), pp. 55–62. Brunschvicg had thought the order and classifications of the First Copy to be the work of the Port-Royal editors (*OBP* I, pp. III–IV), an opinion Michaut had previously pronounced probable in his edition of the *Pensées* (Fribourg: 1896), p. LXXXIII.

There is good reason to hold that the Table of Contents found in both Copies (and whose order both respect) is the work of Pascal himself (see note 21 below). I find this to be the strongest argument that one of the Copies represents the order of Pascal's papers as they were found at his death. (See note 19 below for a discussion of the claims of the First and Second Copies to reflect that order.) Topliss, however, is skeptical of the Pascalian origin of the Table and other features of the First Copy (*The Rhetoric of Pascal*, pp. 159–164).

18 Lafuma worked according to the theory that Pascal had been interrupted in his work of classifying all of his materials for the Apology into the twenty-seven *liasses à titres*. Consequently, in his editions of the first type (Paris: Delmas, 1948, 2 vols; 1952, 1 vol; 1960, 1 vol.), he puts each of the "unclassified" fragments that, in his opinion, belongs to the Apology in one of the *liasses à titres*. Thus he "completes" Pascal's classification. But in his editions of the second type (Paris: Éditions du Luxembourg, 1951, 3 vols; Paris, Club de Meilleur Livre, 1958, 2 vols; Paris, Éditions du Seuil, Collection Livre de Vie, 1962, 1 vol., and OC the following year), he follows the order of the First Copy.

19 My reasons for preferring the Second Copy are as follows:
1) Unlike the First Copy, which bears corrections by multiple hands and many traces of the work of decipherment, the Second Copy is a fair copy, a finished product which the Périer family kept at home for its own reference. Given the Périer's scrupulosity with regard to Pascal's papers, it seems reasonable to believe that the order of their personal reference copy would be the definitive one.
2) More important, the unities of the Second Copy (1–27 and I–XXXV) "bridge" notebooks. Consequently, the order of the notebooks which compose it is inalterable. This shows that the order of the Second Copy was considered to be definitive from the beginning.

On the contrary, in the First Copy each unity is written on a separate material unity, e.g., a notebook or a *feuille double*. This means that the order of the unities 1–27 and I–XXXIV could be changed at will. In fact, some of them were circulated separately to certain of the Port-Royal editors. The present arrangement of the First Copy was not made permanent until 1715 when it was bound somewhere in the Limousin.

Lafuma, referring to the two Copies, says: "Quel est donc le manuscrit qui a conservé l'ordre qui existait à l'origine? Pour notre part, nous fixerions notre choix sur le 12449 [the Second Copy]." *Recherches pascaliennes*, p. 77. Why then did he base his editions on the First Copy?

The status of the First and Second Copies and the hypothesis of a Third are discussed in some detail by Mesnard in "Aux origines de l'édition des 'Pensées': les deux copies," in *Les Pensées de Pascal ont trois cents ans* (Clermont-Ferrand: G. Bussac, 1971), pp. 1–30. Philippe Sellier's Introduction to his edition of the *Pensées* (Paris: Mercure de France, 1976) should also be consulted.

20   Cf. Mesnard, *LPP*, pp. 32–38.

21   There is no autograph Table of Contents, yet the Table must be Pascal's work. It appears three times — twice in the First Copy and once in the Second. Very many of its titles are found in the autograph material on separate fragments which must have rested on top of *liasses à titres*; therefore, we may infer that the titles in the Table are Pascal's. But is the *order* of the titles in the Table (and consequently the order of the *liasses à titres* corresponding to them) also the work of Pascal? The answer must be affirmative given that in all three exemplars of the Table we find a) exactly the same sequence of titles and division of titles into (unequal) columns, b) one title deliberately crossed out but left legible, and c) another title scrupulously listed even though there is no *liasse* corresponding to it. It is impossible to attribute b) and c) to the invention of the Port-Royal editors, else they would not appear in the Second Copy, the fair copy. Therefore, the Table must be the work of Pascal as regards both the titles and their arrangement.

Jean Mesnard notes additional arguments on behalf of the Table's Pascalian origin in *LPP*, pp. 26–30.

22   Why does the Table appear twice in the First Copy? See Mesnard, *LPP*, p. 35.

23   "Introduction" to *Pensées*, tr. by A.J. Krailsheimer (Harmondsworth, Middlesex, England: Penguin Books, 1967), p. 21.

24   Additional "internal evidence" is provided by *pensées* 149, 402 and 482. The last two are lists of "proofs." Number 149 seems to be a kind of *aide-mémoire* for Pascal's talk at Port-Royal (the fragment is entitled "A. P. R."). It does not deal with the "proofs," however.

25   The *Vie de M. Pascal* and the *Préface* may be found in OC. References to them are to page numbers of OC. The *Discours* and the relevant

169

section of *Traité de l'éducation d'un prince* may be found in vol. XII of Brunschvicg's OBP. References to them are to page numbers of that volume. (Vol. XII contains the *Vie* and *Préface* as well.)

26 G. Périer, *Vie de M. Pascal*, p. 24. Nicole, *Traité de l'éducation d'un prince*, p. CCXLI, attributes to Pascal a preference for proofs from nature over metaphysical proofs. But the example he gives of the former — a proof of the immateriality of the soul from the inability of matter to think — seems as much metaphysical as physical.

27 This talk was given in 1658. É. Périer's *Préface* was written in 1669 and the *Discours* was penned between 1667 and 1668.

28 É. Périer, *Préface*, p. 495; Filleau, *Discours*, pp. CCII—CCIII.

29 Filleau, *Discours*, pp. CCVI—CCVII.

30 I have consistently put quotation marks around this word because Pascal uses *"preuve"* in a wide sense. He does not mean by it a demonstration *more geometrico* but simply a good argument, i.e., one which gives reasonable even if not conclusive grounds for accepting a conclusion. "The prophecies, even the miracles and proofs of our religion are not of such a kind that they can be said to be absolutely convincing, but they are at the same time such that it cannot be said to be unreasonable to believe in them" (P #835; cf. #840). Many have erred in thinking that Pascal held the "proofs" to be conclusive, even if only to someone antecedently well-disposed to them. Hugh Davidson includes God's touching of the heart (*inspiration*) and habit (*la machine, coutume*) among the "proofs." *The Origins of Certainty* (Chicago: 1979), p. 146, n. 12. However, this is not in accord with #808 where the proofs, perceived by reason, are contrasted with habit and *inspiration*.

31 Filleau, *Discours*, p. CCX.

32 *Ibid.*, p. CCXVII; É. Périer, *Préface*, p. 496.

33 Filleau advances some arguments for the trustworthiness of the Old Testament narrative on pp. CCXV—CCXVIII. Cf. also CCVII.

34 But according to Annie Barnes, "Les allusions au pari dans le *Discours* sont nombreuses sinon précises" and "l'idée du pari se dessine à deux moments très précis" in Étienne's *Préface*. See "La Conférence à Port-Royal et les Liasses de Pascal," *French Studies*, 10 (1956), p. 235. I do not find a reference to the wager in any of the passages in question.

35 Cf. especially P #34.

36 This word is a translation of *divertissement*, a term often rendered as "diversion." Diversion does suggest turning aside (here, from what is essential), and as the Apology's *point de départ* it makes a neat opposition to conversion, its intended goal. Nonetheless, it is too suggestive of innocent pastimes. Another possibility would be "escape." The man who distracts himself is *fleeing* from boredom and from confrontation with the essential, final questions concerning life and death.

37 This fragment is not found in the *liasse* "Distraction" although it clearly deals with that theme. I have therefore cited it at this stage of the argument since this makes for clarity of exposition. I have followed the same procedure in other cases as well.

38 See P #427 for a scathing indictment of the indifferent.

39 Cf. P #136.

40 This is part of the *exposé* of man's wretchedness without God mentioned in #6. The picture of the unbeliever's misery without God becomes complete once Pascal has shown him man's natural unfitness for knowing (cf. nos. 44, 45 and 48) and the sham character of merely human virtue, especially justice (nos. 60 and 86), as well as the hollowness of human institutions (nos. 26, 44, 977). The complementary notion of God as the only true source of happiness for man is discussed fairly fully in #148.

41 It is Nature which should keep us from being skeptics. It does not allow us to really believe that we might be dreaming now, etc. "Nature confounds the skeptics and Platonists" just as they confound the dogmatists (#131).

42 It is not clear whether or not God is a "first principle" of the kind meant here even though he too is perceived by the heart (#424). The fact that he is known by the heart makes rhetoric, always an important part of apologetics, doubly important for Pascal. In the long run, he must incline the unbeliever's heart toward God. Unfortunately, the apologist alone cannot do this. The most he can do is persuade the unbeliever to give intellectual assent, and then to habitually live the truths of the faith. Habit may eventually fit him to receive the grace which, if it is forthcoming, will result in God being known through the heart. This is faith, and it alone saves.

43 Of course, if the unbelievers are theists of another sort (e.g., Muslims), then this step in the argument will not be necessary. The Apology seems to be addressed primarily to nontheists in Christian lands, however.

44 I am treating the wager as meant to establish belief in *a* God who will only later be identified as the Christian God. My reasons are as follows. First of all, the wager does not work as an argument for the Christian God. As is obvious, there is no more reason to wager on him than on any other deity who promises his faithful eternal rewards. Secondly, I think that an analysis of the fragment *"Infini-rien"* shows that this is what Pascal intended. Nowhere in the formulation of the wager is "God" indentified as the Christian God. Just prior to the exposition of the argument Pascal twice affirms that we can know *that* God is without knowing *what* He is. And finally, the very first words of the argument proper (after "Parlons maintenant selon les lumières naturelles") are: "S'il y a un Dieu il est...." "If there is *a* God." The indefinite article is most instructive. For further discussion see my "The Role of the Wager in Pascal's Apologetics," *The New Scholasticism*, LVII, No. I, Winter 1983.

45 Surprisingly, the wager is considered by many to be based on the threat of perdition as well as or even instead of the hope of eternal happiness. For example, P.T. Landsberg states that "He [Pascal] envisaged a God who would exact severe retribution from anyone who ordered his life as if he did not exist." "Gambling on God," *Mind*, 80, (1971), p. 101. As a matter of fact, the wager does not contain a word about hell or retribution although it is *sous-entendu* that he who does not wager on God will not be rewarded by him. However, there are passages in the *Pensées* in which Pascal does allude to the risk of punishment run by those who live as though God did not exist. Cf. nos. 158, 427 and 428.

46 In "The Will to Believe," William James raises the objection stated in n. 44 as well as the further one that the belief inspired by the wager is of such a selfish, calculating kind that it could hardly be supposed to be efficacious for salvation. It has also been asserted that the wager should not be made because it is irretrievable. It may be a good bet, but if you lose you are unable to wager again and thus you have no hope of recouping your losses. Cf. Topliss, *The Rhetoric of Pascal*, p. 196.

47 If, after the wager is made, you still have trouble believing, Pascal advises you to make a habit of Christian practices. Habit tames the passions and will, it is hoped, make you better disposed to receive the grace only God can give. Cf. 808 and the end of 418. This would be Pascal's answer to the criticism of James in the preceding note. That is, the calculation of the wager is at best only a first step to genuine faith, a gift of grace, and salvation.

48 This inference is not drawn by Pascal but I have supplied it to strengthen the argument. It is certainly consonant with what he says about God's duties to man in #840 and it might be said to follow from it.

49 P nos. 203–222.

50 Many critics have echoed the sentiment of Voltaire who, in the last of his *Lettres philosophiques*, called Pascal a *"misanthrope sublime."* However, Pascal is also a *"philanthrope sublime"*; he insists on man's *grandeur* every bit as much as on his *bassesse*.

51 Cf. P #446 and the end of 449.

52 Pascal's "Lettre à Mlle. de Roannez," fin d'octobre 1656 (p. 267 in OC), should be consulted on the Hidden God in addition to the *Pensées*.

53 Some have held that prophecies were more important than miracles as "proofs" in Pascal's view. The first line of #335 seems to verify this. The resolution is simple. The miracles were the chief "proof" in Christ's day because the prophecies had not yet been fulfilled, and indeed they called for miracles. Since in our day we see no or very few miracles, the fulfillment of the prophecies, itself a miracle, is the greatest "proof" for us now.

54 Voltaire, in the last of the *Lettres philosophiques*, makes the natural rejoinder to this odd claim. Men do not need the help of truth to fall into error; they are quite capable of doing it on their own.

55 This argument is taken from the second of fourteen *pensées* found by Jean Mesnard and published in *Blaise Pascal, textes inédits* (Paris: Desclée de Brouwer, 1962). Obviously, it presupposes the historical reliability it is supposed to show. Pascal takes it as given that Shem, Lamech, etc., were real men who actually lived very long lives.

56 *Les Pensées de Pascal* (Paris: Larousse, 1972), p. 213.

1 Karl Jaspers quotes Nietzsche as saying: "Where my critics are concerned, I am often under the impression that they are scoundrels. Not *what* is said, but that *I say it* and what should have made me in particular arrive at it — only that seems to interest them . . . They judge me in order to ignore my work: they explain its genesis, and thereby consider it adequately *disposed of.*" *Nietzsche: An Introduction to the Understanding of His Philosophical Activity*, tr. by Charles Wallraff and Frederick Schmitz (South Bend: 1979), p. 7. The reference is to *Nietzsches Werke* (Leipzig: 1904), XIX, p. 360.

2 Ronald Hayman, *Nietzsche: A Critical Life* (New York: 1980), p. 1.

3 "Foreword" to *Philosophy and Truth: Selections from Nietzsche's Notebooks of the Early 1870's*, tr. and ed. by Daniel Breazale (New York and Sussex: 1979), p. viii.

4 Nietzsche's notion of the *Übermensch* is not terribly distinct, but in general one may say that he is noble, lofty of spirit, and perhaps most important he is radically autonomous, a value-creator, a law unto himself. In his hardness and greatness of spirit he says "Yes!" to life no matter what terrors it may hold. He is a *briseur d'obstacles* who delights in enemies worthy of himself. He is master of himself.

 Did Nietzsche conceive of the Overman as something *beyond* man or as something essentially of humankind, although a high development thereof? There are passages which suggest each interpretation. For example, see Z–V 3 and A 3.

5 This notion is of course a common one in the nineteenth century, but Nietzsche also shares with the young Hegel an insistence on the reason-stultifying character of religious upbringing as well as the contention that, after Jesus's death, Christianity became a new Judaism. Had Nietzsche read *The Positivity of the Christian Religion*?

6 R.J. Hollingdale makes this point in Appendix D of his translation of *Twilight of the Idols and The Anti-Christ* (Harmondsworth, Middlesex, England: Penguin Books, 1968), p. 193.

7 Cf. *Selected Letters of Friedrich Nietzsche*, ed. and tr. by Richard Middleton (Chicago and London: U. of Chicago Press, 1969), p. 326 and p. 345.

8 For Nietzsche's delusions of succeeding God see the letters to Jacob Burckhardt (Jan. 4 and 6, 1889) on pp. 345—47 of *Selected Letters* and the fragment on p. 800 of *Basic Writings of Nietzsche*, ed. and tr. by Walter Kaufmann (New York and Toronto: 1966).

9 GM I 15. The quotation from Aquinas, cited in Latin by Nietzsche, is an accurate paraphrase of *Summa Theologiae* III, Supplementum, Q. 94, Art. 1. But a look at the context of Nietzsche's citation shows that Aquinas has been grossly misrepresented. There, it is made quite clear that the blessed do not delight in the sufferings of the damned *as such* (a point made again in Q. 94, Art. 3), but that they delight in the heightened awareness of their own bliss that the sight of the damned produces through contrast. "And thus divine justice and their freedom [from punishment] will be the *per se* causes of the rejoicing of the blessed, but the punishment of the damned the cause *per accidens*." No malice is required for this. One need only recall these famous words of Lucretius: "Sweet it is, when on the great sea the winds are buffeting the waters, to gaze from the land on another's great struggles; not because it is pleasure or joy that anyone should be distressed, but because it is sweet to perceive from what misfortune you yourself are free." *De Rerum Natura*, II, 1—4 (Bailey's translation).

As for Tertullian, with a little imagination one might well wonder whether he was a Christian to gratify a pre-existing animus towards those in power or whether, because he was a Christian and hence a member of a viciously persecuted sect, he was less than benignly disposed to the mighty of the earth.

10 *Ibid.* Nietzsche cites the original Latin of Tertullian's *De Spectaculis*, ch. 29. The translation appearing above is that of the Rev. S. Thelwall in *The Ante-Nicene Fathers*, vol. III (Grand Rapids: 1957).

11 Nietzsche occasionally, almost grudgingly, admits that slave morality has not been a total disaster. "Human history would be altogether too stupid a thing without the spirit that the impotent have introduced into it." ". . . But it is only fair to add that it was on the soil of this *essentially*

175

dangerous form of human existence, the priestly form, that man first became an *interesting* animal, that only here did the human soul in a higher sense acquire *depth* and become *evil*. . . ." (GM I 6, 7) It is odd that rendering the human spirit interesting and less stupid should not count as an enhancement of the type man, and that the comparative stupidity and uninterestingness of the masterful man should not count as an objection to him.

12 This process is analyzed at some length in the very canny second essay of GM.

13 Arthur Danto, *Nietzsche as Philosopher* (New York: 1965), pp. 164–165. "Moral optics" — that is, the optics of value — is a Nietzschean concept and a very important one. See especially W–Ep.

14 Plato, *Gorgias*, 483b. Translation by W.D. Woodhead.

15 Indeed, "Rome" has rattled its chains on a number of occasions. Nietzsche saw the Renaissance as the reawakening of the noble ideal and Napoleon as that ideal made flesh. Both, however, were sabotaged by the Germans. They blighted the Renaissance through Luther, who *restored* the Church at the very moment it was undone by secularism, humanism, and venal popes, and they opposed Napoleon with their "Wars of Liberation." Cf. EH–W 2.

16 In spite of Nietzsche's insistence that he is not a meliorist, it is hard to see how a man who seems to feel "permanently condemned to the repellent sight of the ill-constituted, dwarfed, atrophied and poisoned" (GM I 11) could *not* wish to improve his neighbors.

17 The physician metaphor breaks down when one sees what Nietzsche has in mind for the "patients": "The weak and ill-constituted shall perish: first principle of *our* philanthropy. And one shall help them to do so" (A 2; cf. G IX 36).

18 Similarly, Nietzsche held that Paul was so eager to head a movement that would supersede Judaism because of his frustration at being unable to live up to the Jewish law (M 68).

176

1 For information on Nietzsche's slender knowledge of modern languages, including French, see Kurt Weinberg's "The Impact of Ancient Greece and of French Classicism on Nietzsche's Concept of Tragedy," *Studies in Nietzsche and the Classical Tradition*, eds. James O'Flaherty, et al. (Chapel Hill: University of North Carolina Press, 1976), p. 90. Nietzsche's reading of seventeenth-century French authors, including Pascal, is concisely discussed therein. The appreciation of Nietzsche's French is based on C.A. Bernoulli's *Franz Overbeck Und Frederick Nietzsche*, 2 vols., (Jena: 1908), I, p. 154.

2 James Robert Dionne, *Pascal et Nietzsche* (New York: Burt Franklin, 1974), p. iii. A list of Nietzsche's direct references to Pascal is found in Appendix III (pp. 81–94).

3 U I, pp. 61–62. Distraction also appears in U III, pp. 144–145. (Page references are to the Levy translations.) Cf. also M 22 which seems to show the influence of Pascal on "*la machine*."

4 "It is extremely significant that he [Nietzsche] never seriously discusses the arguments Pascal brings to show the truth of Christian doctrine. Like Voltaire, he believes that the 'pari' is Pascal's main argument, and the last third of the *Pensées*, which deals with the 'preuves,' is not considered. Nietzsche is not interested in such things. He is like Pascal's interlocutor, who follows him up to the 'pari,' but in this case is not brought by that argument to desire to pursue the search on Pascal's lines. And, as Pascal says, such a person may read and re-read the 'preuves' without their having any effect on him. . . . But Nietzsche has parted company intellectually with Pascal at the 'pari' − he is not fundamentally concerned whether one or other 'system' is objectively true . . . but only with the relative effects of the 'systems' on the personality of the believer and the history of our kind. This explains why a man of Nietzsche's intellectual integrity can go so far with Pascal and yet deny him to the end." W.D. Williams, *Nietzsche and the French* (Oxford: Basil Blackwell, 1951), p. 161. This puts the matter neatly, although I think that Williams is

wide of the mark when he credits Pascal with the view that "without faith there can be no 'proof'."

5 Cf. p. 50 above, and cf. esp. n. 44 to Chapter One.

6 For Nietzsche's idea of the Eternal Recurrence see esp. FW 341. It springs from *amor fati*: because one loves fate, one wants nothing different from what has happened. In fact, he who loves and affirms even only one event loves and affirms them all since all events are indissolubly bound together. And the highest mode of affirmation is to will that one event, along with all others since they are inextricably linked to it, shall recur again and again, forever. Kaufman lists Nietzsche's references to *amor fati* in his translation of WM (p. 536, n. 95). And, as he correctly points out in his *Nietzsche: Philosopher, Psychologist, Antichrist* (Princeton: 1974, 4th ed.), p. 327, Nietzsche propounds the Eternal Recurrence as a true cosmological hypothesis only in his unpublished notes. In his published works, which must be taken as definitive of his views, he says, not that all events *will* eternally recur, but only that the greatest life-affirmer would *want* them to.

7 See E.R. Dodds, *Pagan and Christian in an Age of Anxiety* (New York and London: 1970), p. 33, n. 4.

8 As Henri Birault says, "Cet amour [of Nietzsche for Pascal] est donc comme l'amour du maître d'art devant une beauté ruinée." "Nietzsche et le pari de Pascal," *Archivio di Filosofia*, 1962, III, p. 87.

9 *Selected Letters*, p. 327. The letter is dated Nov. 20, 1888.

10 *Nietzsche and the French*, p. 58.

11 Jean Guitton, *Génie de Pascal* (Mayenne: 1962), p. 26.

12 Perhaps, as Professor Kurt Weinberg has suggested to me, this passage should be taken *cum grano salis*. It could be mock self-depreciation by a violently anti-Wagnerian ex-Wagnerian meant to devalue a Wagnerian pamphlet written in a period of youthful folly.

13 See the first paragraph of Kant's splendid little essay "What is Enlightenment?"

Chapter Four

1 Of course, in some cases the evidence for a conclusion may lie precisely in the circumstances in which the conclusion came to be believed. "The Hessians are coming! The Hessians are coming!" "Is this true?" "Yes, George told me he saw them, and he's never been known to touch the bottle or tell a lie."

2 See note one to Chapter Two.

3 J.P. Stern, *A Study of Nietzsche* (Cambridge University Press, 1979), p. 147.

4 One suspects that this is the tacit basis of most Christian belief, and it has often been the explicit basis as well. For example, St. Louis (King Louis IX) stoutly affirmed that it was reasonable to believe even if only on "hearsay" from one's elders. Cf. Ch. One of Joinville's *Histoire de Saint Louis*, p. 216 in *Historiens et Chroniqueurs du Moyen Age* (Bibliothèque de la Pléiade, 1952). It is translated in *Chronicles of the Crusades* by M.R.B. Shaw (Harmondsworth: Penguin, 1963).

5 Pascal uses *"témoin"* in a sense broad enough to include the Old Testament prophets as well as Jesus' contemporaries and near contemporaries. Cf. nos. 592 and 615.

6 Since Gibbon, there has been a vast literature on the relation of early Christianity to Roman Culture. Adolph Harnack's *The Mission and Expansion of Christianity in the First Three Centuries* (London: 1908, 2nd ed. tr. by J. Moffatt; German editions in 1902, 1906, 1915, 1924), is still quite valuable, and E.R. Dodds' *Pagan and Christian in an Age of Anxiety: Some Aspects of Religious Experience from Marcus Aurelius to Constantine* (Cambridge University Press, 1965), is invaluable for the period it treats. A small sample of sound and readable recent work would include Robert M. Grant, *Early Christianity and Society: Seven Essays* (San Francisco: Harper and Row, 1977), and *Augustus to Constantine: The Thrust of the Christian Movement into the Roman World* (New York and Toronto: Harper and Row, Fitzhenry and Whiteside, 1970); Henry Chadwick, *Early Christian Thought and the Classical Tradition* (Oxford

University Press, 1967); and R.A. Markus, *Christianity in the Roman World* (New York: Scribner's, 1974). In particular see Dodds, Ch. One, for pagan attitudes toward the material world and pagan *Weltschmertz* and lack of vitality; Grant's "Christian Devotion to the Monarchy" in *Early Christianity* for the attitude of the early Christians to the civil authorities; Chadwick and Dodds (esp. Ch. Three) for affinities between pagan and Christian thought; and Harnack for a concise account of the grudging esteem accorded the early Christians even by their opponents (pp. 211–213 and 265–269). The picture which emerges is not that of GM I.

7 Dodds, pp. 120–121.

8 John Wilcox, *Truth and Value in Nietzsche: A Study of his Meta-Ethics and Epistemology* (Ann Arbor: U. of Michigan Press, 1974), p. 198.

9 *On the Standard of Taste and Other Essays* (Indianapolis: 1965), p. 7.

10 Cf. G. Périer, *Vie de M. Pascal* , pp. 27 and 32.

11 Thomas Babington Macaulay, *The History of England* (Boston and New York: 1899), X vols. Vol. V, pp. 190–191 (xvii). Originally published in V volumes from 1848–1861, in London.

12 See, for example, George Allen Morgan's *What Nietzsche Means* (Cambridge, Mass.: 1941), p. 36; Hans Kung, *Does God Exist?* tr. by E. Quinn (New York: 1980), p. 403; and Stern, p. 147. Kaufmann, on the other hand, insists that Nietzsche's atheism is not an axiom but the result of his commitment to parsimony of axioms (pp. 100–101). However, the passage (EH II 1) he cites in support of this view is immediately preceded by these words which he does *not* cite: "I do not by any means know atheism as a result; even less as an event."

13 Cf. pp. 90 and 108 above for citations from M 91 and 95. Cf. also J 21, MA I 133 and M 90.

14 "Not even as a child" is very dubious autobiography. See, for example, Hayman, pp. 38–39. At any rate, it is certain that, for the mature Nietzsche, belief in these things was never what William James calls a "live option."

15 One might be tempted to defend Nietzsche's assumption of atheism on rhetorical grounds. After all, his announcement of the Death of God (FW 125) is a proclamation of rampant atheism. Thus, he may have felt

justified in taking disbelief as a premise his readers shared. Or, he may have been addressing himself only to potential higher men; they would doubtless be atheists anyway.

But this will not do. There is no reason for thinking that potential higher men are already atheists. In fact, Nietzsche specifically states that what is worst in Christianity is that it attacks and destroys strong souls — Pascal, for example (WM 252). And if one thinks that disbelief is really almost universal, why write book after book, diatribe after diatribe against Christianity? Who would write Philipics if he thought there was no Philip?

16 "The ass arrived, beautiful and most brave." The "ancient mystery" of which Nietzsche speaks is of course the Mass, since these words are said to have figured in a special Mass in medieval Verona. It was to honor the ass which bore the Holy Family to refuge in Egypt. Voltaire pokes fun at this in the article "Âne" in the expanded version of his *Dictionnaire Philosophique*. Perhaps Nietzsche encountered it there.

17 Cf. FW 344, GM III 24 and Z II 12. Wilcox's book is the best general treatment of Nietzsche's epistemology. Hans Vaihinger's classic *Die Philosophie des Als Ob* (Leipzig: 1911; English translation New York, 1924) should also be consulted. Breazale presents an interesting selection of material from the Nachlass in *Philosophy and Truth*.

18 "Nietzsche is prepared to resign himself unreservedly to this passion [for unlimited truth]; he is able to silence all objections springing from consideration of what is necessary or conducive to life.. . ." Jaspers, *Nietzsche*, p. 201. Kaufmann, basing his interpretation on FW 344, affirms that faith in the god-like character of truth is Nietzsche's faith, and that Nietzsche considers himself to be "still pious" for this reason. But Kaufmann's view is untenable. As Arthur Danto points out (p. 191 n.), Kaufmann fails to cite the last part of the passage; there Nietzsche calls the value of truth into question. Kaufmann's largely irrelevant reply to Danto can be found on pp. 358–359 of his *Nietzsche*.

19 Cf. J 1, 2 and 5; cf. also the passages cited at the beginning of n. 17 above.

20 Nietzsche is not alone in the willingness to subordinate truth to value of some sort. Some members of the opposition have felt the same way, which is not surprising, and have said so, which is. Schopenhauer draws our attention to the following remark of a professor of philosophy, a Herr Bachmann: "If a philosophy denies the reality of the fundamental ideas of Christianity, it is either false, or, even if true, it is nevertheless useless." *The World as Will and Representation*, tr. by Payne (New York: 1968), vol. I, p. 512 n. 49.

21 See FW 110 and 111 and WM 507. The chapter "Perspectivism" in Danto's book is helpful on Nietzsche's pragmatic theory of truth. For an evaluation of Nietzsche's theory of truth more favorable than mine see Bk. Two, Ch. Two of Jasper's *Nietzsche*.

22 Danto recognizes this although he thinks that "The inconsistency is not so much in his thought as in his language" (p. 80). Kaufmann is well aware of the seriousness of the problem; he discusses it (pp. 204—207) in the context of the problem with the Will to Power raised in the text above. He suggests, as a way of defending Nietzsche, a position which holds that the human mind might be so constituted that it must interpret the cosmos as fundamentally composed of Will to Power. A Kantian move of this sort would make it necessary to construe the universe as Nietzsche does, i.e., as Will to Power, but it would not force Nietzsche to claim that he was giving a true description (in the correspondence sense) of the character of the real. However, as Kaufmann points out (p. 207), the claim that the human mind is constituted in this way seems to be empirically false. And, one might add, this claim is not to be found in Nietzsche.

23 J 36. The concept of the Will to Power was at first extended only to living things. "Only where there is life, there is also will: not will to life but . . . will to power" (Z II 12). However, it was later extended to non-living things as well. See the chapter "The Discovery of the Will to Power" in Kaufmann's *Nietzsche*.

24 Cf. FW 110 and 111. It is awkward to have a pragmatic theory of truth which possesses its truth in the correspondence sense, but one could imagine a situation even more awkward: a correspondence theory of truth affirmed as true for pragmatic reasons. In the former case, which

appears to be Nietzsche's, one would be forced to admit that one's theory of truth did not hold for all propositions. For example, Nietzsche would appear committed to the view that propositions such as "Evaluations are made when truth claims are made" are true in the correspondence sense. But consider the latter case, one whose theoretical interest is perhaps greater. Suppose it were shown that the correspondence theory of truth were the one most useful for life. Then adherents of Nietzsche's pragmatic theory would be forced to affirm the correspondence theory as true. But if they affirm the correspondence theory of truth as true, they should abandon their allegiance to a pragmatic truth-criterion. Yet it was on pragmatic grounds that they adopted this new theory which now bids them *not* decide truth claims on pragmatic grounds. So, what is the status of their allegiance to the correspondence theory now?

25 J.S. Mill, *Sedgwick's Discourse* in *Collected Works* (Toronto and Buffalo: 1963 –), XIX vols. Vol. X, p. 57.

26 See the opening paragraph of "Utility of Religion" in *Three Essays on Religion*, Vol. X, p. 403.

Chapter Five

1 This account owes something to Breazale's discussion of Nietzsche's "philosopher of tragic knowledge" and "philosopher of desperate knowledge." See pp. xl–xli.

2 First of all, there is no reason why the correspondence could not be understood as being between our propositions and Kant's phenomenal realm (things as perceived by us). But suppose it were held that *real* truth-about-the-world would entail a correspondence between propositions and the in principle inaccessible realm of things-in-themselves

(noumenal reality), and hence that truth-about-the-world was of course unattainable?

The problems with such a claim stem from the well known difficulties with Kant's doctrine of noumenal reality. We do not *know* that there is such a realm; it might be that phenomenal reality is the only reality. A noumenal realm is of course *possible*, but since we can never know that (let alone what) it is, there is no reason to postulate it. Totally unknowable, it is totally lacking in explanatory power and otherwise needless, and so Ockham's Razor may fairly lop it off.

Danto (p. 96) is sensitive to the problems posed by the Kantian undercurrents in Nietzsche's epistemology.

3   Cf. Dodds, pp. 121–24, cited in part above on p. 112, and Harnack, pp. 219–240. Some of the relevant texts they note are Celsus, *True Word*, I ix, xii, xxvi; Lucan, *Peregr.* xiii; Galen, *Peri Diaphoras Sphugmon*, II iv; and Marcus Aurelius, *Meditations*, 11.3.2. Justin Martyr makes reference to the prophecies to counter the objection that Christians believe on mere assertion (e.g. *First Apology* I 30), but the charge seems to have been largely accurate. According to Harnack, "At bottom the faith required was a blind faith. Still, it would be a grave error to suppose that for the majority of people the curt demand that authorities must be simply believed and reason repudiated, acted as a serious obstacle to their acceptance of the Christian religion. In reality, it was the very opposite. The more peremptory and exclusive is the claim of faith which any religion makes, the more trustworthy and secure does that religion seem to the majority. . . . The most welcome articles of faith are just the most paradoxical, which are a mockery of all experience and rational reflection; the reason being that they appear to guarantee the disclosure of divine wisdom and not of something which is merely human and therefore unreliable" (pp. 222–223).

4   That these doubts are Pascal's and not those of some imaginary interlocutor of the sort found in the wager is clear from the avowal "I have wished a hundred times over. . . ." The *libertin*, long sunk in *divertissement*, would not be able to say this.

5   "Gradually it has become clear to me what every great philosophy so far has been: namely, the personal confession of its author and a kind of

involuntary and unconscious memoir. . . ." (J 6) "Whoever rejoices in great human beings will also rejoice in philosophical systems, even if completely erroneous." *Philosophy in the Tragic Age of the Greeks* (South Bend: 1962), tr. by Marianne Cowen, p. 23.

6 Breazale, p. 63.

7 *Heauton Timorumenos* (The Self-Tormentor), 77. "I am a man, and I consider nothing human alien to me."

8 Karl Jaspers, *Nietzsche and Christianity* (Chicago: 1961), tr. by E.B. Ashton, pp. vii–viii.

9 Kung, p. 415.

10 It is precisely this imagination that Nietzsche enjoins on Christians in M 61. "*The needful sacrifice.* – These serious, excellent, upright, deeply sensitive people who are still Christians from the very heart: they owe it to themselves to try for once the experiment of living for some length of time without Christianity, they owe it to *their faith* in this way for once to sojourn 'in the wilderness'. . . . Only if you are driven back, not by homesickness but by *judgment* on the basis of a rigorous *comparison*, will your homecoming possess any significance!"

Appendix

1 See note three to Chapter Five.

2 Pierre Bayle, for example, found the objection to God from evil unanswerable from a rational point of view. See especially the articles "Manicheans" and "Paulicians" and the Second Clarification in his *Dictionnaire Historique et Critique* (1697). All three are included in Richard Popkin's translation of selections (Indianapolis: 1965). More recently, John Mackie has found evil to be a decisive objection to the rationality of Christian belief. See "Evil and Omnipotence," *Mind* (64), 1955.

3 "The God that Paul created is the negation of a God." Nietzsche, *The Anti-Christ*, 47.

4 Arguments proceeding to show that something is entailed by or incompatible with "God" presume that the concept of God used would be an accurate description of God if he existed. But in point of fact, our ideas of God are to a great extent *stipulations* regarding what we would like to see counted as divine.

Thus, Descartes, in the First Meditation, saw no problem in entertaining the hypothesis that God might be a deceiver; at that point in his argument he needed powerful grounds for skepticism. But then in the Third Meditation, when that hypothesis would no longer do, it suddenly dawned on him that divinity and deceitfulness were incompatible. Until the early twentieth century, Christians saw little problem with the doctrine of hell. But we are more humanitarian and more opposed to pain on principle than were our forebears, especially if the pain is understood as retribution rather than correction. And so it is not surprising that, like John Hick in *Evil and the God of Love* (New York: 1966), pp. 341–345, many Christians have rejected the doctrine of hell because they find it inconsistent with a God of love. One can only marvel, then, at the obtuseness of Augustine, Aquinas, Pascal, Dr. Johnson and so many others reputed to be of some intellect — even though they all believed that "God is love," they didn't notice that hell was impossible, that a God of love who allows it is a *contradictio in adjecto*. Were they really so poor at *logic*?

5 For example, John Stuart Mill, though not himself a Christian, reasoned from the limited perfection of the world that a "god" probably existed who was not omnipotent. See "Theism" in *Three Essays on Religion* (1874), especially pp. 451–453 in vol. X of his *Collected Works*.

6 The most celebrated attempt in this line is of course Leibnitz's characterization of God's omnipotence in the *Theodicy* (1710). Owing to inherent defects in the natures of the finite things of which a universe would be constituted, God is limited as to the total amount of perfection that he can impart to a universe.

7 Bayle is inexorable in cataloguing the divinely willed iniquities recounted by the Scriptures. Of his many articles dealing with Old Testament

186

immoralities, "David" is the most famous. According to Popkin in the Introduction to his edition of Bayle, Bayle's contemporary Pierre Jurieu affirmed, as part of an explanation as to why the faith appears anti-rational and anti-moral, that the Scriptures would seem divine only to one illumined by grace (p. xxvi). More recently, Mill has labelled the Christian God's reluctance to divulge himself and his maintenance of hell as particular moral enormities. Indeed, "of the moral difficulties and perversions involved in revelation . . . there are some of so flagrant a character as almost to outweigh all the beauty and benignity and moral greatness which so eminently distinguish the sayings and character of Christ." X, p. 424, "Utility of Religion." Mark Twain's posthumous *Letters from the Earth* (New York: 1962) is a more popular recital of divine immoralities.

8 Other skeptical commonplaces focus on the immorality of God as represented by Christian philosophers and theologians. For example, Calvin's insistence on the absolute predestination of both the elect and the reprobate, and Augustine's claim that unbaptized infants suffer damnation (albeit of a mild sort) present a God who seems, by any human standard, quite unjust. Of course, logically speaking, the believer could deny that God must be just or demand that the definition of "justice" be revised for God. The former, however, is wildly heterodox, an abandonment rather than a defense of faith. As for the latter, a definition of justice sufficiently latitudinarian to accomodate such apparent divine malfeasance would seem to constitute, not a revision, but an inversion of universally recognized norms of justice. Small wonder, then, that when Dante confronts the obvious injustice of God's dam-nation of virtuous pagans who, having lived in lands the Gospel never reached, perforce died unbaptized, he falls to depreciating and abusing the human intellect (*Paradiso*, XIX, 27–90). The logical structure of these "intra-framework" objections is, of course, the same as that of the problem of evil, and the difference lies in the latitude which orthodoxy allows the believer in his formulations of divinity and its attributes.

9 Clement's *Exhortation to the Greeks*, Tertullian's *Apologeticus* and Augustine's *City of God* may serve as examples of this ubiquitous motif

in early Christian polemics. Needless to say, the immorality of the classical pagan deities had already been roundly denounced by thinkers such as Xenophanes and Plato.

10 C.S. Lewis, *Surprised by Joy* (New York: 1955), pp. 235–236.

11 Augustine, *Confessions*, V 24.

12 From a purely logical point of view, Augustine's objections to Manicheanism could have been overcome in the same manner as his objections to the Old Testament, i.e., by construing the offending passages figuratively. For example, he was troubled by the empirical falsity of Manichean astronomy (*Conf.* V 3–9), but he *could* have rejoined: "These celestial bodies, physical things, are but figures for spiritual ones," or "Mani's purpose was to teach us how to go to heaven, not how the heavens go." In sum, the choice between Manicheanism and Catholicism seems to have been made less on strictly logical grounds than Augustine himself quite realized.

13 Soren Kierkegaard, *Fear and Trembling and The Sickness unto Death* (Princeton: 1968), tr. by Walter Lowrie, p. 35. *Fear and Trembling*, in which the citation above appears, was first published in 1843.

14 Unwillingness on the part of many Christians to consider that anything *could* count decisively against the faith, insistence that any difficulties with it must be *merely* apparent, might help explain the impatience of many anti-Christian writers with the question of the "truth of Christian belief."

15 "So great has been the power of religion to persuade men to evil." *De Rerum Natura*, I 101.

16 Others might include the traditional claim that God is altogether simple (*"omnino simplex"* in Aquinas, *ST* Ia 3, 7) yet a trinity; the actual presence of two apparently contrary natures, divine and human, in the person of Christ; and the Roman Catholic doctrine of the Real Presence, implying as it does the "multi-location" of the body of Christ.

17 The way in which Aquinas deals with this problem is instructive. To the objection that there cannot be generation of the Word within the godhead because every generated thing *receives* its *esse* from its generator and thus cannot be, as the Word must be, *per se subsistens*, he replies: "non omne acceptum est receptum in aliquo subjecto; alioquin non

posset dici quod tota substantia rei creatae sit accepta a Deo, cum totius substantiae non sit aliquod subjectum receptivum. Sic igitur id quod est genitum in divinis accipit esse a generante non tamquam illud esse sit receptum in aliqua materia vel subjecto, quod repugnat subsistentiae divini esse; sed secundum hoc dicitur esse acceptum inquantum procedens ab alio habet esse divinum, non quasi aliud ab esse divino existens. In ipsa enim perfectione divini esse continetur et verbum intelligibiliter procedens et principium verbi, sicut et quaecumque ad ejus perfectionem pertinent, ut supra dictum est" (*ST* Ia 27, 2).

"Not everything which is accepted is received in some subject, otherwise it could not be said that the whole substance of a created thing is accepted from God," that is, since the created thing *accepts* its *all* from God, there is no prior existing subject to *receive "tota substantia."* Hence not all *acceptance* of *esse* is *reception* of *esse*. But this presupposes that creatures are made *out of nothing*. In short, the defense of the crucial contention that not everything which is accepted is received in some subject rests on the possibility of creation *ex nihilo*, i.e., grant one mystery and another can be explained.

Further, the fact that receiving existence is not compatible with divinity does not mean that accepting existence is. It simply begs the question to say that what is generated in God "insofar as it proceeds from another has divine existence." The *possibility* of proceeding from another and yet having divine existence (being *per se subsistens*) is precisely what needs to be shown.

18 "It is a mystery, but not a falsehood."

19 This is, in effect, what some contemporary theologians have done. For example, Kung considers the Incarnation to be the "making flesh" of God's Word and Will, but *not*, properly speaking, of God himself. Thus, for Kung Jesus Christ is the "Son of God" but not God (*Does God Exist?* pp. 680–691, 699–702). This view of things is rationally consistent, and it is easier to defend than the traditional view that Jesus was the Second Person made flesh and that the Second Person is *homoousios* with the First, the Father. But, leaving aside the Scriptural warrant for Kung's views, there is a problem posed by such radical revisions that I do not think has been fully addressed. The proponents of such revisions,

in maintaining their superiority to Christian doctrine as traditionally interpreted, are in the position of saying to believers: "Our pardon; we, your teachers, have for centuries propagated doctrines which we now see to be radically inexact. Pray disregard our previous impassioned asseverations of their verity. Now we have got things right at last. Trust us." But how worthy of trust, of faith, would a source like this, whether theologians or church, be?

There have been Christians who fully expected that, as time passed, doctrine and dogma would radically evolve. For instance, the Dunker Michael Welfare told Benjamin Franklin that "it had pleased God to enlighten our minds so far, as to see that some doctrines which we once esteemed truths were errors, and that others which we had esteemed errors were real truths. From time to time he has been pleased to afford us farther Light, and our Principles have been improving." *Autobiography* (New York: 1981), p. 146. And so the Dunkers, rightly realizing that their beliefs of today might not be those of tomorrow, refused even to commit the principles of their faith to writing.

20 See the first pages of Bayle's Third Retraction in the *Dictionary*, pp. 421–423 in Popkin's edition. To take on faith that any objections to the faith are ultimately answerable has been, at least in Catholic circles, a frequent admonition to laymen. Thus, they need not be troubled if they are at a loss for answers. And so Saint Louis told the chronicler Joinville: "No one, unless he is a very fine clerk, should dispute [with unbelievers]. But the layman, whenever he hears the Christian religion slandered, should not defend the Faith but with his sword – and that he should stick in his opponent's belly, and as far as it will go." *Histoire de Saint Louis*, Ch. One, p. 219 in the Pléiade edition. Miguel de Unamuno was taught in catechism class to say: "Do not ask me the reason of that, for I am ignorant. Holy Mother Church possesses Doctors who will know how to answer you." *Tragic Sense of Life*, tr. by J.E.C. Flitch (New York: 1954), p. 76. But is it only proper humility should the Doctors wish to affirm that what is unreason from a merely human perspective must be reason from God's, i.e., *ignoramus et ignorabimus*?

21 I will let Russell's and Grelling's antinomies (often mislabelled "paradoxes") serve to illustrate set theoretic and semantic antinomies, respectively.

190

A set, as Georg Cantor intuitively described it, is a collection of objects of thought (numbers, sets) or of perception (trees, bricks). Some sets are members of themselves, e.g., the set of all non-trees is itself a non-tree and so contains itself as a member. Some sets are not members of themselves, e.g., the set of all trees is not itself a tree and hence is not a member of itself. We should therefore be able to construct a set S which is the set of all sets that are not members of themselves. But, unhappily, this set involves a contradiction. We have only to ask: "Is S a member of itself?" If the answer is "yes," then S violates its own description, for it may contain *only* sets that are *not* members of themselves. If the answer is "no," a contradiction is likewise generated, for S must contain *all* sets that are not members of themselves.

Grelling points out that words may be true of themselves, e.g., "English" is an English word, or not true of themselves, e.g., "German" is not a German word. Terms of the first type he calls autological; those of the second, heterological. But is the term "heterological" heterological? If so, it has the property it designates and so it is *not* heterological after all. If not, it lacks the property it designates and so it *must be* heterological.

Almost any intermediate or advanced work in symbolic logic, theory of sets or foundations of mathematics deals with the antinomies of set theory. James Cargile's *Paradoxes: A Study in Form and Predication* (Cambridge Univ. Press, 1979) is a thorough discussion of the principles underlying semantic antinomies.

I find the clearest example of an antinomy in metaphysics to be the argument for the existence and non-existence of a necessary being (the subject, in the *Critique of Pure Reason*, of Kant's Fourth Antinomy.)

Granting the eminently plausible claim that nothing can exist unless there is a sufficient reason for its existence, then — contrary to the law of the excluded middle — it can be the case neither that all beings are contingent nor that at least one being is necessary (non-contingent).

The claim that all beings are contingent must be false since then there would be no *sufficient* reason for the existence of any contingent being. For, since the *raison d'être* of any contingent being ("x") can only involve other contingent beings, and since each of these requires a sufficient reason for *its* existence, complete responsibility for "x's" existence

191

cannot be assigned. That is, there is no complete (sufficient) reason (or condition) for "x's" existence. But this, *ex hypothesi*, is impossible.

Nor can a being be necessary. Such a being would either have to be its own condition (reason) for being, and hence logically prior to itself (which does not seem possible), or without a condition for its existence and hence in violation of our initial hypothesis, "the principle of sufficient reason."

22 In *Skeptical Essays* (Chicago: 1981), Benson Mates argues persuasively that previous attempts to resolve the Liar's and Russell's antinomies have failed dismally, and that the problems the antinomies pose are genuine, deep and possibly intractable.

This is an important book. Too often the antinomies are viewed as significant only for their immediate context. Mates, however, realizes their wider implications for epistemology and in particular for skepticism. With regard to that topic, one can only wonder what Descartes' reaction would have been to contradictions deduced from premises "clearly and distinctly" perceived to be true.

23 In a recent article, Alvin Plantinga uses Russell's antinomy to call the veracity of self-evidence into question. See pp. 21–27 of "Is Belief in God Rational?" in *Rationality and Religious Belief*, ed. by C.F. Delaney (Notre Dame, 1979). It is part of an attempt to show that there is no reason not to take the existence of God as axiomatic ("basic") in one's conceptual scheme.

Of course, the veracity of self-evidence could be questioned on other grounds as well. Might it be the constitution of our minds, and not the nature of the known, that causes certain types of propositions to appear self-evident to us? Is it possible that certain drugs would affect what appears self-evident to us by their presence or absence? If we knew, as Descartes thought that he did, that we were fashioned by a God who is not a deceiver, then (as Plantinga notes) we might affirm that God would not let us be mistaken about propositions whose self-evident verity extorted our assent. But in the absence of such knowledge, why should we suppose that, simply because a proposition has a certain effect on us, it must be true? Unless one wishes merely to define such propositions as true, their truth is very much an article of faith.

SELECT BIBLIOGRAPHY

I Nietzsche

Andler, Charles. *Nietzsche: Sa Vie, Sa Pensée*. 10th ed. 6 vols. Paris: Éditions Brossard, 1931.

Copleston, Frederick, S.J. *Friedrich Nietzsche: Philosopher of Culture*. 2nd ed. New York and London: Barnes and Noble and Search Press, 1975.

Danto, Arthur. *Nietzsche as Philosopher*. New York: Macmillan and Co., 1965.

Deleuze, Gilles. *Nietzsche et la Philosophie*. Paris: Presses Universitaires de France, 1962. 4th ed. 1975.

Frenzel, Ivo. *Friedrich Nietzsche: An Illustrated Biography*. Translated by Joachim Neugroschel. New York: Pegasus, 1967.

Hayman, Ronald. *Nietzsche: A Critical Life*. New York: Oxford University Press, 1980.

Heidegger, Martin. "Nietzsche's Wort 'Gott ist tot'" in *Holzwege*. Frankfurt am Main: Klostermann, 1950.

Hollingdale, R.J. *Nietzsche: The Man and His Philosophy*. London: Routledge and Kegan Paul, 1965.

————. *Nietzsche*. London and Boston: Routledge and Kegan Paul, 1973.

Jaspers, Karl. *Nietzsche: An Introduction to the Understanding of his Philosophical Activity*. Translated by Charles F. Wallraf and Frederick J. Schmitz. Tucson: University of Arizona Press, 1965. German editions in 1936, 1947.

Kaufmann, Walter. *Nietzsche: Philosopher, Psychologist, Antichrist*. 4th ed. Princeton: Princeton University Press, 1974.

Kung, Hans. *Does God Exist*? Translated by Edward Quinn. New York: Doubleday, 1980. Nietzsche and Pascal are both treated in some depth and are occasionally considered together.

Morgan, George Allen Jr. *What Nietzsche Means*. Cambridge: Harvard University Press, 1941.

Nietzsche, Friedrich. *Gesammelte Werke, Musarionausgabe*. 23 vols. Munich: Musarion Verlag, 1920–1929.

———. *Werke: Kritische Gesamtausgabe*. Edited by Giorgio Colli and Mazzino Montinari. Berlin: Walter de Gruyter, 1967ff.

———. *The Complete Works of Friedrich Nietzsche*. 18 vols. Edited by Oscar Levy. New York: Macmillan, 1909–1911; reissued New York: Russell and Russell, 1964.

———. *Basic Writings*. Translated and edited, with commentaries, by Walter Kaufmann. New York: Random House, 1966. This collection includes *The Birth of Tragedy, Beyond Good and Evil, On the Genealogy of Morals, The Case of Wagner* and *Ecce Homo*.

———. *The Portable Nietzsche*. Translated and edited by Walter Kaufmann. New York: The Viking Press, 1954. This contains *Twilight of the Idols, The Antichrist, Nietzsche Contra Wagner* and *Thus Spoke Zarathustra* as well as selections from earlier works and letters.

———. *The Gay Science*. Translated, with commentary, by Walter Kaufmann. New York: Random House, 1974.

———. *The Will to Power*. Translated by Walter Kaufmann and R.J. Hollingdale. New York: Random House, 1968.

———. *Thus Spoke Zarathustra*. Translated by R.J. Hollingdale. Harmondsworth: Penguin, 1961.

———. *Twilight of the Idols and The Anti-Christ*. Translated by R.J. Hollingdale. Harmondsworth: Penguin, 1968.

———. *Daybreak: Thoughts on the Prejudices of Morality*. Translated by R.J. Hollingdale. Cambridge: Cambridge University Press, 1982. Also known as *The Dawn*.

———. *Selected Letters of Friedrich Nietzsche*. Edited and Translated by Christopher Middleton. Chicago and London: University of Chicago Press, 1969.

———. *Philosophy and Truth: Selections from Nietzsche's Notebooks of the Early 1870's*. New Jersey and Sussex: Humanities Press and Harvester Press, 1979.

Reichert, Herbert W., and Schlechta, Karl. *International Nietzsche Bibliography*. Chapel Hill: University of North Carolina Press, 1960; revised and expanded in 1968.

Schlechta, Karl. *Der Fall Nietzsche*. München: Carl Hanser Verlag, 1959.
Stern, J.P. *A Study of Nietzsche*. Cambridge: Cambridge University Press, 1979.
Wilcox, John. *Truth and Value in Nietzsche: A Study of His Metaethics and Epistemology*. Ann Arbor: University of Michigan Press, 1974.
Williams, W.D. *Nietzsche and the French: A Study of the Influence of Nietzsche's French Reading on his Thought and Writing*. Oxford: Basil Blackwell, 1952.

II Pascal

Barnes, Annie, (ed.). *Écrits sur Pascal*. Paris: Éditions du Luxembourg, 1959.
Courcelle, Pierre. *L'Entretien de Pascal et Sacy, ses sources et ses énigmes*. Paris: J. Vrin, 1960.
Davidson, Hugh. *The Origins of Certainty*. Chicago: University of Chicago Press, 1979.
Goldmann, Lucien. *Le Dieu caché*. Paris: Gallimard, 1959; reprinted 1972.
Guitton, Jean. *Génie de Pascal*. Mayenne: Aubier, 1962.
Hubert, Sr. Marie Louise, O.P. *Pascal's Unfinished Apology: A Study of His Plan*. Port Washington, N.Y., and London: Kennikat Press, 1973. Originally published at New Haven: Yale University Press, 1952.
Lafuma, Louis. *Recherches pascaliennes*. Paris: Delmas, 1949.
————. *Controverses pascaliennes*. Paris: Éditions du Luxembourg, 1952.
————. *Histoire des Pensées de Pascal (1656–1952)*. Paris: Éditions du Luxembourg, 1954.
LeGuern, M. et M.R. *Les Pensées de Pascal: De l'anthropologie à la théologie*. Paris: Librairie Larousse, 1972.
Lhermet, J. *Pascal et la Bible*. Paris: J. Vrin, 1931.
Mesnard, Jean. *Pascal*. Paris: Desclée de Brouwer, 1965. Translated by Claude and Marcia Abraham. University: University of Alabama Press, 1969.
————. *Les Pensées de Pascal*. Paris: SEDES Réunis, 1976.

195

Mesnard, Jean. "Aux Origines de l'édition des 'Pensées': les deux copies" in *Les Pensées de Pascal ont trois cents ans*. Clermont-Ferrand: G. Bussac, 1971.

Pascal, Blaise. *Oeuvres de Blaise Pascal, publiées suivant l'ordre chronologique, avec documents complémentaires, introductions et notes.* Edited by Léon Brunschvicg, Pierre Boutroux and Félix Gazier. XIV vols. Paris: Hachette, 1904–1921. Reprinted by Kraus Reprint, Ltd. Vaduz: 1965. Vol. XII contains Filleau's *Discours*, Étienne's' *Préface* and Gilberte's *Vie de M. Pascal*.

———. *Oeuvres Complètes*. 1 vol. Edited by Louis Lafuma. Paris: Éditions du Seuil, 1963.

———. *Oeuvres Complètes*. Edited by Jean Mesnard. Paris: Desclée de Brouwer, 1964ff. Vols. I and II have appeared so far; vol. V will contain the *Pensées*. This edition contains a wealth of important historical and biographical material.

———. *Pensées*. Edited by Philippe Sellier. Paris: Mercure de France, 1976. This edition follows the order of the Second Copy.

———. *Pensées*. Translated by A.J. Krailsheimer. Harmondsworth: Penguin, 1966. This edition follows the order of Lafuma's *Oeuvres Complètes*, the order of the First Copy.

———. *Provincial Letters*. Translated by A.J. Krailsheimer. Harmondsworth: Penguin, 1967.

Steinmann, Jean. *Les trois nuits de Pascal*. Paris: Desclée de Brouwer, 1963.

Topliss, Patricia. *The Rhetoric of Pascal: A Study of His Art of Persuasion in the Provinciales and the Pensées*. Amsterdam: Leicester University Press, 1966.

Wetsel, David. *L'Ecriture et le Reste*. Columbus: Ohio State University Press, 1981.

III Comparative Studies

Bauer, Henry. "Pascal et Nietzsche." *La Revue Germanique*, Jan./Feb., 1914. Sketch of a never-completed doctoral thesis. Published posthumously by Henri Lichtenberger.

Birault, Henri. "Nietzsche et le pari de Pascal." *Archivio di filosofia*, 1962—1963, pp. 67—90.

Dionne, James Robert. *Pascal et Nietzsche*. New York: Burt Franklin and Co., 1974. Their views of asceticism are seen as central.

Léveillé-Mourin, Geneviève. *Le langage chrétien, anti-chrétien de la transcendance: Pascal et Nietzsche*. Paris: J. Vrin, 1978. As the title suggests, language is the principal focus of attention.

Lohmann, Elise. *Nietzsche und Pascal*. Inaugural Dissertation. Leipzig, 1909.

Larry Goldberg

A COMMENTARY ON PLATO'S *PROTAGORAS*

American University Studies:
Series V, Philosophy. Vol. 1
ISBN 08204-0022-X   350 pp.   pb./lam., US $ 33.70
Recommended prices – alterations reserved

In this commentary the author presents a reading of Plato's *Protagoras* with a special concern for the fact that the work is a dialogue. He shows how the intentions of both Socrates and Protagoras, and the specific dramatic circumstances, affect the discussion concerning the teachability of virtue. Mr. Goldberg contends that in order to grasp the order of the arguments about the unity of virtue, Athenian education and democracy, continence, and hedonism, one must consider all the seemingly casual incidents and interchanges. In particular, he sees in Socrates' ironic analysis of a poem of Simonides a response to the famous speech of Protagoras which contains the sophist's version of the Promethean creation myth. The differences between sophistry and philosophy are clarified, and Socrates emerges as the dutiful citizen doing his best for democratic Athens.

Contents: A detailed analysis of Plato's *Protagoras:* Socrates – Championing philosophy – Debates Protagoras – The relativistic sophist – About the teachability and unity of virtue and the education suitable for democratic Athens.

PETER LANG PUBLISHING, INC.
34 East 39th Street, USA – New York, NY 10016

Daniel H. Frank

THE ARGUMENTS 'FROM THE SCIENCES' IN ARISTOTLE'S *PERI IDEON*

American University Studies:
Series V, Philosophy. Vol. 2
ISBN 0-8204-0035-1   151 pp.   pb./lam., US $ 15.25
Recommended prices – alterations reserved

The *Peri Ideon* is Aristotle's first and most sustained critique of Platonic metaphysics. Arguments for the existence of Forms are presented; then Aristotle develops critical objections. This study is concerned with the first set arguments in the *Peri Ideon,* the so-called arguments 'from the sciences'.

Contents: Introduction – Text, translation, and notes to translation – The three Platonic arguments 'from the sciences' – Interim conclusion – Aristotle's two objections – Summary and conclusion – Notes and bibliography.

Gerard Casey

NATURAL REASON

A Study of the Notions of Inference, Assent, Intuition, and First Principles in the Philosophy of John Henry Cardinal Newman

American University Studies:
Series V, Philosophy. Vol. 4
ISBN 0-8204-0078-5   347 pp.   hardcover/lam., US $ 37.–
Recommended prices – alterations reserved

Natural Reason is an examination of the religious epistemology of Cardinal Newman. Although his epistemology was developed primarily to defend the rationality of religious belief, it is, nevertheless, pertinent to problems of belief in general. The theme of the work is that Newman's central notions conceal crucial ambiguities. These are the result of his inheriting an inadequate philosophical tradition whose limitations make it exceedingly difficult for him to give systematic expression to his thought. The removal of these ambiguities will allow Newman's thought to reveal itself in all its lucidity.

Contents: Inference – Assent – Intuition – First Principles – Argument – Rationality – Religious Belief – John Henry Cardinal Newman.

PETER LANG PUBLISHING, INC.
34 East 39th Street, USA – New York, NY 10016

Michael J. Zimmermann

AN ESSAY ON HUMAN ACTION

American University Studies:
Series V, Philosophy. Vol. 5
ISBN 0-8204-0122-6   335pp.   pb./lam., US $ 31.–
Recommended prices – alterations reserved

An Essay on Human Action seeks to provide a comprehensive, detailed, enlightening, and (in its detail) original account of human action. This account presupposes a theory of events as abstract, proposition-like entities, a theory which is given in the first chapter of the book. The core-issues of action-theory are then treated: what acting in general is (a version of the traditional volitional theory is proposed and defended); how actions are to be individuated; how long actions last; what acting intentionally is; what doing one thing by doing another is; what basic action is; and what omitting to do something is. Attention is also given to the concepts of causation, intention, volition, deciding, choosing, and trying. Finally, a libertarian account of free action is tentatively proposed and defended.

Contents: Three theories: of events; of human action; of free action.

PETER LANG PUBLISHING, INC.
34 East 39th Street, USA – New York, NY 10016